Signs, Trails, and Wayside Exhibits
Connecting People and Places
Third Edition

By Michael Gross, Ron Zimmerman,
and Jim Buchholz

Schmeeckle Reserve, Wisconsin

UW-SP FOUNDATION PRESS, INC.
UNIVERSITY OF WISCONSIN-STEVENS POINT
STEVENS POINT, WI 54481

Signs, Trails, and Wayside Exhibits: Connecting People and Places

By Michael Gross, Ron Zimmerman,
and Jim Buchholz

Third Edition, 2006

UW-SP Foundation Press, Inc.
University of Wisconsin-Stevens Point
Stevens Point, WI 54481

Printed and bound in the United States of America.

ISBN *(13-digit)*: 978-0-932310-47-7   *(Paperback)*
ISBN *(10-digit)*: 0-932310-47-8   *(Paperback)*
ISBN *(13-digit)*: 978-0-932310-48-4   *(Hardcover)*
ISBN *(10-digit)*: 0-932310-48-6   *(Hardcover)*

**Library of Congress Cataloging-in-Publication
Data**

Gross, Michael (Michael P.)
    Signs, trails, and wayside exhibits : connecting people
        and places / by Michael Gross, Ron Zimmerman,
        and Jim Buchholz. -- 3rd ed.
            p. cm. -- (Interpreter's handbook series)
    Includes bibliographical references and index.
    ISBN-13: 978-0-932310-47-7 (pbk.)
    ISBN-10: 0-932310-47-8 (pbk.)
    ISBN-13: 978-0-932310-48-4 (hardcover)
    ISBN-10: 0-932310-48-6 (hardcover)
1. Sign painting. 2. Signs and signboards--Design
        and construction. 3. Woodwork. I. Zimmerman,
        Ronald. II. Buchholz, James. III. Title.
    TT360.T73 2006
    790.06'9--dc22
                                        2006013562

Cover photo: Big Bend National Park, Texas

Interpreter's Handbook Series

Serving interpretive professionals and students with comprehensive, easy-to-use guidebooks since 1988.

Making the Right Connections: A Guide for Nature Writers (1988)

Creating Environmental Publications: A Guide to Writing and Designing for Interpreters and Environmental Educators (1991)

The Interpreter's Guidebook: Techniques for Programs and Presentations: Third Edition (1994)

Interpretive Centers: The History, Design, and Development of Nature and Visitor Centers (2002)

Signs, Trails, and Wayside Exhibits: Connecting People and Places: Third Edition (2006)

Ordering Books

Visit the Schmeeckle Reserve web site for updated information about the Interpreter's Handbook Series and to order books. All sales support Schmeeckle Reserve and the University of Wisconsin-Stevens Point interpretive program.

http://www.uwsp.edu/schmeeckle

About the Authors

Michael Gross, Ph.D
Professor Emeritus of Environmental
Interpretation

Ron Zimmerman
Director, Schmeeckle Reserve
Instructor of Environmental Interpretation

Jim Buchholz
Assistant Director, Schmeeckle Reserve
Instructor of Environmental Interpretation

Schmeeckle Reserve
University of Wisconsin-Stevens Point
2419 North Point Drive
Stevens Point, WI 54481
Phone: (715) 346-4992
E-mail: schmeeckle@uwsp.edu

Michael Gross   Ron Zimmerman   Jim Buchholz

The authors have developed and co-instructed environmental interpretation classes at the University of Wisconsin-Stevens Point, College of Natural Resources for 30 years. Mike and Ron created the Interpreter's Handbook Series in 1988, a series of training manuals for the interpretive profession. The team serves as a consultant to interpretive agencies and private organizations, facilitating workshops and providing planning and evaluation services. Their enthusiasm for natural history grew from their childhood explorations—Mike in northwest Iowa, Ron in the Nebraska Sandhills, and Jim in Wisconsin state parks.

Interpretive Services

For more information about the Interpreter's Handbook Series and interpretive consulting and design services, visit the Schmeeckle Reserve web site:

http://www.uwsp.edu/schmeeckle

Table of Contents

Acknowledgements

This book was made possible by the generous contributions of many people. Answers, advice, and contributions were offered by scores of friends, colleagues, and clients.

The original examples and contributions of Tanner Pilley still grace the pages of this third edition. We are grateful to him for sharing a lifetime of knowledge and insights acquired in his career with the National Park Service. We thank our colleague, Suzanne Trapp, for her assistance in developing some of the concepts in the first edition of the book. Many of these ideas have evolved in this current edition.

We thank ALUimage, ECOS Communications, the Harpers Ferry Center of the National Park Service, Interpretive Graphics, iZone, Pannier Graphics, Richard Ostergaard, Split Rock Studios, Stone Imagery, and Wilderness Graphics for graciously sharing their professional perspectives and practical examples of design and fabrication. We appreciate the many individuals who shared photographs and information with us.

We were blessed with the finely tuned proofreading and editorial skills of Sunshine Buchholz who spent tenacious hours improving the readability of this text.

Wyalusing State Park, Wisconsin

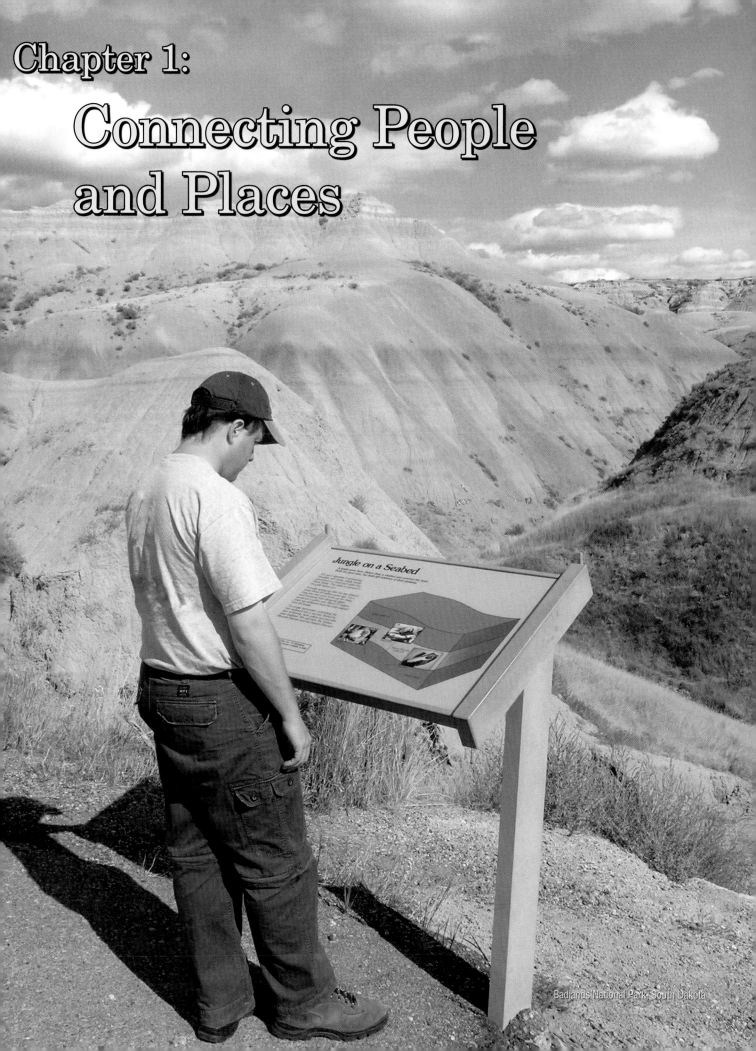

Chapter 1:
Connecting People and Places

Badlands National Park, South Dakota

The Crowley's Ridge Experience

*A*s I drove across the flat fields of the Arkansas Delta, I was surprised to see a long snaking ridge on the horizon. Highway signs for the "Crowley's Ridge Nature Center" caught my attention and I decided to investigate.

An attractive stone entry sign assured me that this was the right place, and set my expectations for the experience... I was going to see wildlife.

A roofed kiosk greeted me from the parking lot. Welcome signs en-

ticed me by describing Crowley's Ridge as "one of the most unique landforms in the world."

A map of the site showed a short trail loop around a pond, which looked like a perfect place to see wildlife. Animal tracks punched into the metal sign supports reinforced my anticipation.

An information bulletin board displayed the hours the site was open, some important rules, and special programs and events.

The trail started on a nature center deck high above the pond... what a great view! A boardwalk meandered along the ridge with several observation points, before sloping down to the water's edge.

Signs along the trail described different species of wildlife in provocative ways. I touched life-size models of a water snake, turtle, frogs, and prairie seeds. I pressed buttons to hear the calls of various frog species... and a real frog answered.

I compared the difference between the feet of waterbirds that I saw on the pond. And I felt oversized models of water bugs.

The meandering trail, beautiful views, encounters with wildlife, and unique signs helped me to understand and appreciate this amazing place.

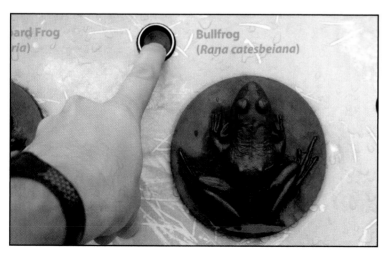

Making Connections

Signs, trails, and wayside exhibits are connectors. They give meaning to the experience of the moment. As at all interpretive sites, the real experience at the Crowley's Ridge Nature Center is outside of the building. Effective trails and signs are important components for telling the story of a site.

At the Crowley's Ridge Nature Center, you are invited to walk the trail and "discover." It is a sensory experience: the sights, smells, and sounds of Crowley's Ridge. It is an intellectual and emotional experience: from the dramatic views of the pond to encountering wildlife up-close. The wayside exhibits provide hands-on experiences that appeal to diverse audiences, while enhancing their understanding of wildlife on the Ridge.

Harmonious Design

Harmonious design is key in the success of Crowley's Ridge Nature Center. Unity is achieved through the telling of the thematic story of wildlife on Crowley's Ridge. Nature center exhibits, oral programs, and publications are important to expand on this theme, but the trail walks and wayside exhibits link the story directly to the place.

The designs are also unified. Signs share the same fonts, layouts, vivid colors, supports, and metal wildlife cutouts. The design elements were carefully chosen to be friendly and inviting.

Crowley's Ridge Nature Center, Arkansas

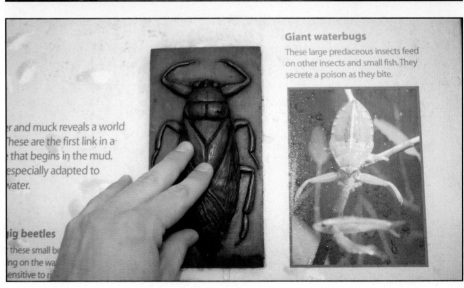

Giant waterbugs
These large predaceous insects feed on other insects and small fish. They secrete a poison as they bite.

r and muck reveals a world
hese are the first link in a
that begins in the mud.
especially adapted to
vater.

ig beetles
these small be
ng on the wa
nsitive to r

Crowley's Ridge Nature Center, Arkansas

Principles for Success

In 2005, the Habitats Nature Trail at the Forrest L. Wood/Crowley's Ridge Nature Center received a Media Award from the National Association for Interpretation. The project illustrates several principles for creating effective signs, trails, and wayside exhibits.

As site managers and interpreters, we are custodians of the people's cultural and natural heritage. We connect them to their legacy. Signs, trails, and wayside exhibits can help make those connections.

Wayside exhibits and signs are part of a larger whole.

They are methods for experiencing a site and learning its stories. They seldom provide detailed or in-depth information, but they can provoke visitors to want more. Audio-visual programs, interpreter-led presentations, brochures, and books provide detail more appropriately to interested visitors.

The site manager must choose media that best meet the needs of visitors at that site. An interpretive plan for the site helps guide these decisions.

Interpretation should always be based on a unified theme.

What is important about your site? Why has it been set aside? Though you may have many possibilities, choose a theme that reveals the meaning of the site to visitors. Each sign or wayside exhibit should fit into that theme.

Learning is best when it is closely associated with the experience.

Wayside exhibits and signs provide information about real things. Their purpose is to interpret concrete objects and experiences on the site.

Wayside exhibits and signs should be harmonious with the site.

They should enhance the on-site experience, not detract from it. Selection of materials, proper placement, and design requires sensitivity and forethought. The worst trail panel or wayside exhibit is an irrelevant, incomprehensible one.

The best interpretation is concise.

The urge to add more subject matter may be strong, but must be resisted. Visitors want to experience the site. They will ignore long, complex messages. A good graphic with a short headline may be all that is needed.

The Habitats Nature Trail was planned and designed by Schmeeckle Reserve Interpreters, Wisconsin and Split Rock Studios, Minnesota in conjunction with the Arkansas Game & Fish Commission. The supports and sculptures were fabricated by Split Rock Studios and the panels by Folia Industries, Quebec.

Interpreting Our Heritage

Well-planned wayside exhibits and trails help visitors discover **meanings** in our resources and sites. This process is called "heritage interpretation."

> Heritage interpretation is a communication process that guides visitors in their search for meanings in objects, places, and landscapes.

Freeman Tilden distilled the essence of interpretation in his classic 1957 book, *Interpreting our Heritage*. He understood the importance of helping people to find relevant and significant connections to our resources. He wrote:

"Information is not interpretation. Interpretation is revelation based upon information."

Meanings develop when visitors are connected both **intellectually** (facts, information) and **emotionally** (feelings, empathy).

Designing trails and wayside exhibits is a creative process that takes into account:
- The interests of our visitors.
- The unique features of our resources and their meanings.
- Effective techniques for connecting visitors to the site.

Meaning-Centered Interpretation Model

Visitors:
- Are autonomous. Choose to read signs or experience trails.
- Are constantly searching for and developing meanings, with or without interpretation.

Resources:
- Have tangible qualities that can be perceived by the senses.
- Shape the meanings that visitors develop.

Signs, Trails and Wayside Exhibits:
- Can serve to connect visitors to the resource and guide the development of meanings.
- Can detract from an experience if not well planned or designed.

Meanings:
- Are more important than information.
- Are ascribed through social norms and cultural values.
- Are intangible and unfixed. No two people experience exactly the same meaning.

The Search for Meaning

"The human mind has evolved to search for meaning."

E.O. Wilson
National Geographic, May 2006

Humans, by nature, seek relevance and meaning in places, objects, and in events. We love to recreate—to spend time with family and friends, to explore exciting places, and to understand the dynamic and confusing world we live in. We recreate to renew our body and mind, but also to rejuvenate our spirit. We celebrate places and events that support our values, cause us to contemplate our beliefs, or that make us feel included in things greater than

Physical resources are *icons*, windows into thoughts, values, and beliefs with multifaceted meanings to different people. Meanings are more important than facts.

our own lives. The desire to find significance in events and landscapes is an innate human need.

Well-planned trails and exhibits can assist visitors in their search for connections to their heritage. In the words of Liberty Hyde Bailey, the Father of American Nature Study, "We must begin with the fact for sure, but the lesson is

not the fact but the significance of the fact." Meanings are more important to people than mere facts. Good interpretation helps visitors find personal connections between tangible places, objects, and events and their own lives and values.

Effective media should grab the interest of visitors and promise them personally rewarding insights into concepts and ideas. The media that we design can open windows of revelation to our visitors who find their own personal meanings in these resources.

Connections on the Oregon Trail

The Oregon Trail was an emigrant road marked by discarded baggage, lost dreams, and graves. Families desperate for new beginnings in the West gambled all they had on the 2000-mile trek across the continent. Many claimed homesteads in Oregon, Washington, and California, but 1 in 10 died on the trail.

Diary quotes and portraits link us to the pioneers of 150 years ago. A simple wayside exhibit creates an opportunity for people to empathize and find meaning in this historic event.

Scotts Bluff National Monument, Nebraska

Emigrant families like this one often stopped to eat and rest near Scotts Bluff in the 1850's.

Wayside exhibit text:

"One woman and two men lay dead on the grass and some more ready to die. Women and children crying, some hunting medicine and none to be found. With heartfelt sorrow, we looked around for some time until I felt unwell myself. Got up and moved forward one mile, so as to be out of hearing of crying and suffering."

John Hawkins Clark, May 13, 1852

Wayside exhibit text:

"Cholera killed more emigrants than anything else on the Oregon Trail. In a bad year, some wagons lost two-thirds of their people. If evenly spaced, there would be at least 10 graves every mile for the 2,000 miles of the trail."

Chapter 2:
Wayside Exhibits and Information Signs

When Native Americans lashed the limbs of this sapling maple to mark a trail, they left a sign for others crossing the vast Horicon Marsh. Signs have always been a basic form of communication.

Just as Native Americans needed direction across ancient wetlands, today's visitors to natural and cultural sites rely on signs and symbols to find their way. Signs inform, warn, guide, identify, and interpret.

Trail Tree, Horicon Marsh, Wisconsin

Planning for Site Signage

Travelers today are moving fast. Motorists make decisions at a glance. Signs for them must be simple and use letters and symbols that communicate quickly. As the visitor's pace slows, signs may become more complex and subtle.

Signs should be deliberately planned to serve all the needs of the visitor as they move through the site. From entrance signs to interpretive signs, each level of signage should be designed to serve a specific purpose.

Types of Signs

A **sign** is an inscribed board, plate, or space that communicates something to the viewer. Signs can be divided into two categories: **information signs** and **interpretive panels**.

Information Signs

Badlands National Park, South Dakota

Willamette National Forest, Oregon

Interpretive Panels and Wayside Exhibits

Crater Lake National Park, Oregon

Information signs provide directions, identification, advertising, warning, rules, or guidance. Each sign presents a single message ("Welcome to Redwood National Park" or "2 miles to Visitor Center").

Common information signs used at natural and cultural areas include:
- Regulation and rule signs (pages 20-22)
- Warning signs (pages 20-22)
- Wayfinding signs
  - Orientation/Maps (pages 23-25)
  - En Route/Directional (page 24)
  - Arrival/Entrance/Site Identification (page 26)
- Traffic signs

Interpretive panels tell the story of a resource, site, or feature. Their primary purpose is to guide visitors to discover meanings. They may have multiple messages and are designed for learning at leisure.

A **wayside exhibit** is an <u>outdoor</u> interpretive panel (versus one found inside a building), or a cluster of interpretive panels and information signs, usually found along trails and roads (wayside) or near significant features. Wayside exhibits include:
- Outdoor interpretive exhibits and signs
- Orientation kiosk exhibits
- Trailhead exhibits
- Information boards (pages 27-29)

Anatomy of a Sign

Sign face

Sign panel

Supports

Cumberland Island National Seashore, Georgia

Each part of an information sign or interpretive panel is important. Signs not only provide information, they also create an impression and set a tone. The three parts of a sign are:

- **Sign face:** Includes all the elements that compose the surface, such as graphics, text, and boxes. See Chapters 3 and 4 for designing effective sign faces.

- **Sign panel:** The physical backboard on which the sign face is inscribed or printed. See Chapter 5 for different types of panel materials.

- **Supports:** Anchor the sign to the site physically and visually. See Chapter 5 for support options.

Why Use Signs?

Signs are commonly used in parks, forests, zoos, aquariums, natural areas, and cultural sites throughout the world to provide information and interpretation. When developing a communication system for your site, consider the advantages and limitations of signs.

Advantages:

- **Signs are user-friendly:** Visitors choose which signs they will or won't read. They also select the amount and detail of information to take in.

- **Signs are always on the job:** As long as your site is open, signs are available to provide visitors with information or interpretation.

- **Signs are economical:** Although design and materials may seem expensive, a wise initial investment will provide years of communication for your site.

Limitations:

- **Signs cannot be made invisible:** They are a human intrusion on the landscape, which may not be appropriate for certain natural or cultural areas.

- **Signs cannot replace a good interpreter:** A sign cannot answer all visitors' questions or respond to spontaneous events.

- **Signs cannot provide complicated or lengthy information:** The majority of visitors will ignore a sign with long text messages, technical writing, and complex ideas.

Wayside Exhibits

A wayside exhibit is an outdoor interpretive opportunity, usually located along a road or trail. It may consist of a single interpretive panel or a cluster of panels that follow a single theme.

One wayside exhibit along the Wildlife Drive in Custer State Park, South Dakota, interprets bison. This is an effective exhibit because:

- Visitors have seen bison along the drive and likely have questions about them.

- It is located at a place where many visitors naturally stop to observe bison grazing.

- It is a safe and convenient place for drivers to stop. The kiosk is off of the main road.

- The design of the panels and kiosk is attractive and fits the rustic theme of the site.

Custer State Park, South Dakota

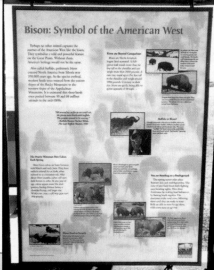

- The interpretation is concise, active, and told through pictures. The following is from the main text:

"Perhaps no other animal captures the essence of the American West like bison. They symbolize a wild and powerful feature on the Great Plains..."

When to Use a Wayside Exhibit

- When it is the best media for a story. Would a roving interpreter or a publication be better? Are those and other options available?

- When there are features or events that need explanation. Would a visitor have questions that would otherwise go unanswered?

- When there are enough visitors to justify the expense of a wayside exhibit.

- When a wayside exhibit does not detract from the site or invite people into a site too sensitive for public use.

- When it is a safe and convenient place for people to stop.

Shenandoah National Park, Virginia

Boulder Creek, Boulder, Colorado

Wayside exhibits should be placed wherever visitors congregate and ask questions.

They can be as simple as a single interpretive sign.

Madison Buffalo Jump State Monument, Montana

Sometimes a story requires more than a single sign. It takes effort to get to Madison Buffalo Jump in Montana, but travelers are rewarded with interesting stories told through a series of panels.

A design reminiscent of traditional Nez Perce motifs is used for this shelter. It houses panels telling the story of White Bird's battle with federal troops. Visitors are offered panoramic views of the battlefield.

Prairie dogs are a popular attraction for travelers in the West. The Grey Cliff wayside uses photochemically etched anodized aluminum panels to explain the life history of the prairie dog.

Resources Connect Visitors to the Story

The most successful wayside exhibits address what can be seen or experienced on the site. Tangible resources can be perceived with the senses, and are power-ful focal points for interpretive signage. The goal of a wayside exhibit is to connect a tangible resource to intangible meanings.

Fort Sumpter, South Carolina

Mt. Saint Helens National Volcanic Preserve, Washington

A crushed car shows the power of the volcanic eruption at Mount Saint Helens. The fence protects it from souvenir hunters. Its presence provokes questions that a wayside exhibit can answer.

A cannon is a tangible artifact of the Civil War.

Glacier Bay National Park, Alaska

A Tlingit canoe brings life to the interpretation of an intriguing culture. The canopy protects it from the region's heavy rainfall.

Black Forest, Germany

A replica of a log raft brings the past to life. Old photographs on the sign help tell the story.

Black Forest, Germany

Foresters in Germany's Black Forest created a wayside exhibit to provoke concern about the effects of acid rain on the forest. It includes informational panels and trees marked to show the progressive decline caused by airborne pollutants.

San Diego Wild Animal Park, California

Visitors to the San Diego Wild Animal Park expect to spend the day. Wayside exhibits are used to develop different storylines and to help visitors understand patterns and relationships.

The xeriscape garden exhibit tells why native vegetation should be used to landscape yards in arid climates.

Temporary and Seasonal Wayside Exhibits

A temporary wayside exhibit is an ideal method for interpreting current or seasonal events. These include:

- Recent research or studies
- Seasonal nesting areas
- Plants or fungi that annually grow in different places

- Daily or seasonal wildlife sightings
- Naturalist program schedules

Schmeeckle Reserve, Wisconsin

Six Mile Cypress Slough Preserve, Florida

Seasonal panels can interpret ephemeral events. Visitors to this wetland learn the spring songs of breeding frogs.

A simple sign can interpret plants that may grow in different places every year.

Lichterman Nature Center, Tennessee

Panels can be fabricated with removable pieces that are switched every season. This system ensures more direct interpretation, while encouraging repeat visitation.

Thematic Art and Wayside Exhibits

"The aim of art is to represent not the outward appearance of things, but their inward significance."

Aristotle

Art is the use of skill and creative imagination to produce an aesthetic object. Its purpose is to connect with people on an emotional and personal level. Every person finds his or her own meaning in a piece of art.

A successful wayside exhibit is essentially a work of art, blending design principles and creativity to tell the story of our site.

Other art forms, like sculptures, poems, and paintings, can enrich a visitor's experience and strengthen the interpretive stories. However, interpreters must be careful to select art that is harmonious with the natural and cultural landscape.

Paintings and Illustrations

Everglades National Park, Florida

Joliet, Illinois

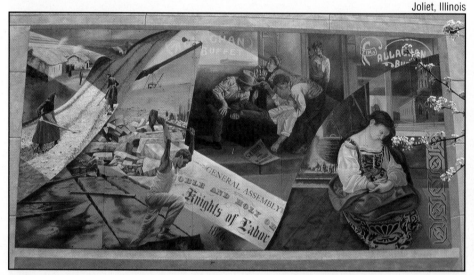

A collage offers an impressionistic view of a hardwood hammock.

A painted scene on the side of a building helps communities celebrate their heritage.

Poems and Quotes

Six Mile Cypress Slough Preserve, Florida

Knockan Crag National Nature Reserve, Scotland

Thematic quotes and poems provoke reflection.

Sculptures

Tome Hill, New Mexico

Bicentennial Park, Illinois

Sculptures at the base of a culturally important hill in New Mexico signify the diverse people who settled the region.

Metal figure silhouettes on the I&M Canal represent historic residents and their occupations.

Beinn Eighe National Nature Reserve, Scotland

Beinn Eighe National Nature Reserve, Scotland

The theme of this trail in Scotland revolves around the Scot's pine. A bench is built with native rock in the shape of a pine seed.

An intriguing rock sculpture in the middle of the trail resembles a Scot's pinecone.

High Desert Museum, Oregon

Little Bighorn Battlefield, Montana

A horse sculpted with barbed wire represents wild mustangs.

Line figures made of metal rods at the Little Bighorn Battlefield unobtrusively recount the experience of Native Americans.

Information Signs: Rules and Warnings

"To the recreation-area manager, rules are purposeful, valuable, and necessary for the proper maintenance of the environment and for the protection of people. Recreationists, however, do not always recognize the worth of rules, because they do not understand them, or simply do not know about them. Better methods are needed to tell what the rules are."

Ross and Mueller
Communicating Rules in Recreation Areas

Recommendations for Rule Signs

• Place rules where visitors are sure to see them. Entrances, bulletin boards, and especially restrooms, give visitors time to read signs.

• Be provocative. Even when placed properly, signs will not be read unless they command attention through colors, graphics, and vivid, concise wording.

• State rules in a direct positive tone. A hostile or dogmatic tone will create resentment and noncompliance. Friendly graphics can support a positive tone.

• Give the reader reasons for the rules.

Bandelier National Monument, New Mexico

Rocky Mountain National Park, Colorado

Olympic National Park, Washington

Information boards at trailheads are commonly used to communicate rules and warnings. They must command attention and appeal for compliance. Read more about information boards on pages 27-29.

Proper placement of signs can reduce destructive behavior.

Rocky Mountain National Park, Colorado

State rules and warnings in simple direct language. People have more respect for rules if they know the reasons for them.

Corkscrew Swamp Audubon Sanctuary, Florida

Aransas National Wildlife Refuge, Texas

Kalalau Trail, Hawaii

San Diego Wild Animal Park, California

Use graphics or universal symbols to enhance understanding.

Rules can be stated in a positive, light-hearted way.

Foxfire Gardens, Wisconsin

San Diego Wild Animal Park, California

Blue Spring State Park, Florida

Everglades National Park, Florida

Kingsley Plantation, Timucuan Preserve, Florida

Aransas National Wildlife Refuge, Texas

Visitors to the Kingsley Plantation are not allowed to touch the historic buildings, but a piece of the wall helps satisfy the temptation.

Be creative, but avoid an accusatory or condescending tone.

Information Signs: Wayfinding

People find their way through unfamiliar places by using visual, audible, and tactile clues. An effective wayfinding plan considers not only signage, but also the architecture, landscape, lighting and landmarks of a site.

The goal of wayfinding is to help people get from one point to another in a positive and reassuring way. Signs stay on the job even when a visitor center is closed. Unified wayfinding signs help ensure that visitors feel comfortable and knowledgeable about your site.

Good wayfinding considers three phases of a visitor's experience.

	Visitor Questions	Types of Wayfinding Signs
Orientation	Where am I now? Where do I want to go? How do I get there?	• Two-dimensional maps • Relief maps • Landmark identification panels
En Route	Am I going the right way? How much further is it? Where do I turn?	• Directional signs • Trail markers • Reinforcement signs
Arrival	Is this the right place? Do I really want to stop here?	• Entrance signs • Facility signs • Site identification signs

Orientation Wayfinding Signs

Rogue River National Forest, Oregon

Roseburg District BLM, Oregon

Maps are commonly used on orientation signs to help visitors visualize where they are within the larger site and how they can travel to other destinations.

Effective map signs include the visitor's current location ("You are here"), distance and travel times, significant landmarks, and accessibility, difficulty, and elevation changes if applicable.

Red Oak Nature Center, Illinois

The Mill of Benholm, Scotland

Orient maps to the site instead of north. "Up" on the map should indicate "straight ahead" from where the visitor is standing.

Significant features (roads, trails, streams, buildings, parking lots, restrooms, landmarks) should be labelled directly on the map, instead of using a reference key. A perspective drawing of the landscape can give visitors a better spatial understanding of the area.

Mosquito Hill Nature Center, Wisconsin

USS Arizona Memorial, Hawaii

Be as direct as possible. This relief carving is rendered to scale and oriented to the landscape.

Rocky Mountain National Park, Colorado

A relief topographic map is a tactile method of quickly orienting visitors to a site.

Scenic vistas are natural locations to orient with landmarks.

Recommendations for Orientation Signs

- Keep maps simple and dramatic.

- Include distance, difficulty, accessibility, and significant features.

- Determine the purpose of the map and avoid trying to show more than that.

- Label key features directly on the map. Avoid using a large number of symbols that require referencing a key.

- Orient the map to the site, not to the compass points. Up on the map should represent "forward" in the site, not necessarily north.

- A "You are here" symbol should be indicated on the map.

- Visible landmarks in the environment should be clearly indicated on the map.

- Maps should be located where they are easily found and most needed (where decisions are made such as trailheads).

- Design the map to complement other wayfinding tools such as signs and color coding systems.

En Route Wayfinding Signs

Brookfield Zoo, Chicago, Illinois

Schmeeckle Reserve, Wisconsin

Schmeeckle Reserve, Wisconsin

Knockan Crag National Nature Reserve, Scotland

En route signs direct visitors and reassure them that they are going the right way. Simple graphics and symbols can convey messages more efficiently than words.

Rustic en route direction signs work well in natural areas.

Unobtrusive signs reinforce that visitors are on the correct route.

Arrival Wayfinding Signs

Salinas Pueblo Missions National Monument, New Mexico

Rogue Gorge, Rogue River National Forest, Oregon

Arrival signs identify an entrance, facility, or site. Successful signs convey a single message, "You have arrived at..."

Arrival signs should be prominent and placed in locations that allow for easy viewing from moving vehicles or over parked cars in a lot.

Petit Jean State Park, Arkansas

Petit Jean State Park, Arkansas

Creative design adds character to a sign, connecting visitors to the stories and feelings of a site.

A unified design plan helps visitors anticipate arrival signs when they are searching for their destination.

Hawaii Tropical Botanical Garden

Pu'uhonua O Honaunau National Historical Park, Hawaii

Information Boards

Information boards, or bulletin boards, are commonly used to communicate current events, rules, trail conditions, naturalist programs, and other temporary or seasonal postings. Without regular maintenance, information boards can become cluttered and unkempt.

An organized and high-quality information board can be an attractive asset to a site, provide clear information to visitors, and enhance their experience.

Black Elk Wilderness, South Dakota

Manatee Park, Florida

A dry erase board *(right panel)* is an inexpensive method for updating daily information, like programs or weather.

Tips for Information Boards

- Organize the board for quick scanning. Use headings, subtitles and symbols. Avoid cluttering the panel.

- Colors and shapes should be interesting and pleasing.

- Use vivid, active language in titles.

- Information should be site-specific and of immediate use to the visitor.

- Information boards should be kept current. Vigorously prune outdated material and replace with current and seasonal events.

Modular Information Systems

Hells Canyon National Recreation Area uses a "Modular Information System" to present information to visitors. In this system, welcome panels, maps, rules, and advisory messages are unified with similar materials, layouts, and design. Every information board contains common elements of design and repetitive components that are organized by color and arrangement.

The boards look professional and organized, and visitors can quickly access the information they need.

Hells Canyon National Recreation Area, Oregon and Idaho

The Hat Point kiosk integrates the modular information board with an interpretive panel about wildfire.

All information boards in the recreational area are unified with the modular system. These include elaborate stone kiosks, simple wooden kiosks, and boards mounted onto the walls of visitor contact stations and restrooms.

Each message is color coded: blue for water-related messages, russet for fire and warnings, and green for camping, trail, and other recreational activities.

Fun poems, unique metaphors, and analogies direct the visitor's attention to important messages. Illustrations introduce and organize messages visually.

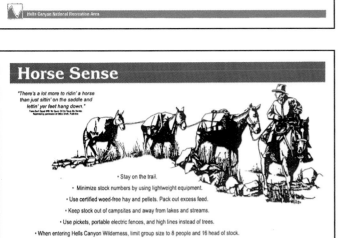

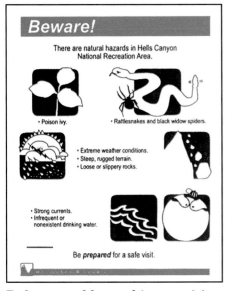

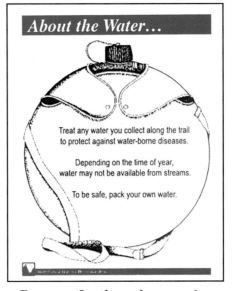

Rules are addressed in a positive tone. Reasons for the rules are given.

Graphics support the message.

Chapter 3:
Sign Design

Lava Tubes

Partially Collapsed Lava Tube

The opposite wall of the Gorge exposes two lava tubes. One, partially collapsed, looks like a cave. The other tube was plugged by a later lava flow. How many separate lava flows can you count?

Lava Flow

Plugged Lava Tube

Lava tubes are formed—

by the rapid cooling of the outer surface of a basalt flow, while the hot lava continues to flow underneath. As the molten lava drains out, it leaves behind a hollow tube.

Sign Faces

Sign Face Components

Fort Rock State Park, Oregon

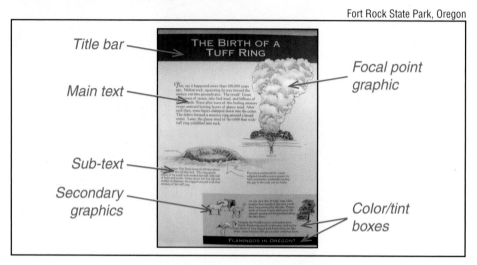

Title bar

Main text

Sub-text

Secondary
graphics

Focal point
graphic

Color/tint
boxes

A sign face greets the visitor and expresses a personality. It is the surface to which the cosmetics of color, type, graphics, and symbols are applied for maximum effect. The goal for designing a sign face is to create a high Fraction of Selection.

The Fraction of Selection

Why do people choose to read or ignore a sign? Simple signs that provoke interest will be selected by more people.

The success of a sign can be viewed as a formula, proposed by Wilbur Schramm as "The Fraction of Selection:"

Low
Fraction of $=\dfrac{\text{Expectation of Reward}}{\textbf{Effort Required}}$
Selection

High
Fraction of $=\dfrac{\textbf{Expectation of Reward}}{\text{Effort Required}}$
Selection

Successful signs increase the expectation of reward and decrease the effort required. The Fraction of Selection is a result of how you craft your message and how you design your sign. Tips for improving messages are in Chapter 4. Tips for design follow.

Badlands National Park, South Dakota

Does this sign have a high or low Fraction of Selection?

- **Low Fraction of Selection:** Requires a great deal of effort to acquire the interpretive message.
- **High Fraction of Selection:** The design and writing encourage and simplify access to the interpretive message.

The Fraction of Selection was presented in The Process and Effects of Mass Communication *by Wilbur Schramm, 1971.*

Inscriptions

Selecting a Typeface

Choosing and placing type on your sign face should not be left to chance. Each typestyle speaks its own language. John Downy, an Iowa artist and sign maker states, "The letters on a sign should demand to be noticed. They need to aggressively catch the eye and hold attention."

Downy provides a rule for text designers: "If a reader says in the process of reading a book, 'Hey, I don't think I've seen this typeface before!' then it is probably a bad typeface. And, if a person can walk by a sign without becoming a reader, it's probably a bad sign."

You don't have to become a master of typography to create effective signs. You just need to learn the basic principles for choosing

a typeface and the spacing and sizing of letters.

Each typeface has its unique personality. Typeface selection handbooks are available online, in libraries, and from local printers. Select a face that expresses the personality you desire.

Font Styles for Signs

Times (abcdefghijklmnopqrstuvwxyz)
Times is a popular serif style used for signs and publications.

Helvetica (abcdefghijklmnopqrstuvwxyz)
Arial (abcdefghijklmnopqrstuvwxyz)
Helvetica and Arial are sans serif fonts with good readability.

Improving legibility with fonts:
- *Avoid script and fancy fonts. Letters are hard to distinguish from one another.*
- Do not mix font styles. It creates disharmony. Instead use *italics*, **bold**, and print size variations for emphasis.

A **serif** is a small cross stroke that adorns the ends of letters in some typefaces. These are often called Roman typefaces from the practice of finishing letters cut in stone with cross-bars.

Sans Serif literally means "without a serif."

Serif vs. Sans Serif

Apostle Islands National Lakeshore, Wisconsin

The National Park Service developed a serif typeface for many of its signs that says "parks are places for leisurely activity, not speedways."

Big Cypress National Preserve, Florida

Highway signs with sans serif typefaces can be read rapidly. This cool, modern typeface conveys little emotion.

Proportion and Size of Lettering

Recommended Type Sizes

Vertical Measurement	Viewing Distance
1/2"	4'
5/8"	6'
2 1/2"	30'
4"	60'

Or for wayside exhibits...

Titles - 72 to 60 point minimum
Subtitles - 48 to 40 point minimum
Body text - 24 point minimum
Captions - 18 point minimum

(Complies with suggested size for visually impaired as per National Park Service recommendations.)

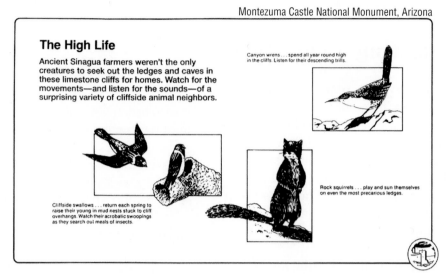

Montezuma Castle National Monument, Arizona

The High Life

Ancient Sinagua farmers weren't the only creatures to seek out the ledges and caves in these limestone cliffs for homes. Watch for the movements—and listen for the sounds—of a surprising variety of cliffside animal neighbors.

Canyon wrens . . . spend all year round high in the cliffs. Listen for their descending trills.

Cliffside swallows . . . return each spring to raise their young in mud nests stuck to cliff overhangs. Watch their acrobatic swoopings as they search out meals of insects.

Rock squirrels . . . play and sun themselves on even the most precarious ledges.

There is a hierarchy of letter sizes on this sign. Their size suggests the order in which the message should be read. They are proportional to each other and to the sign as a whole.

Letter Spacing

Kerning is the process of adding or subtracting space between two letters. Computer desktop publishing programs automatically adjust the space between letters based on their shape. Automatic kerning is not perfect, however, and you may need to manually adjust some spaces.

No Kerning	Automatic Kerning	Manual Kerning
HILLY ACRES	HILLY ACRES	HILLY ACRES
Too much space between the: L and Y A and C	L and Y fit better. Still too much space between A and C.	A and C fit better.

Alignment and Hyphenation

Books, magazines, newspapers, and other printed media often have text **justified**. The right sides of every line in a paragraph line up. However, text for signs should generally be **aligned left with ragged right sides**. This improves reading ease, allows for uniform letter spacing, and is less formal. **Hyphenation** between lines should also be avoided.

Justified with hyphens

You are surrounded by cat-tails, the most abundant plant in the Black River Marsh. Like trees in a forest, cat-tails provide food, cover, and protection for many types of wildlife.

Appropriate for books, magazines, and printed media.

Ragged right, no hyphens

You are surrounded by cattails, the most abundant plant in the Black River Marsh. Like trees in a forest, cattails provide food, cover, and protection for many types of wildlife.

Recommended for signs and wayside exhibits.

Capital Letters and Line Length

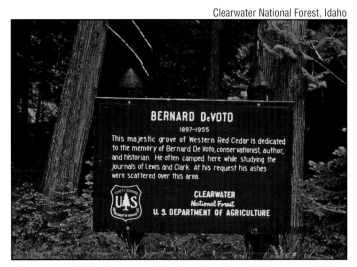

Large blocks of type set in **caps are difficult to read**. A sign set in all caps takes 14% longer to read and takes up 40% more space.

Long lines of continuous text also decreases readability. The longest line on this sign is over 100 characters. Readability is best when the **line length is less than about 60 characters**, or about 8-15 words.

Caps on this sign are limited to headlines, making it more readable.

The lines are also shorter, ranging from 40-45 characters and 8-10 words. This sign has a higher Fraction of Selection and is more likely to be read by visitors.

Open Space

In addition to using all caps, the type crowds this sign face. When words are crowded into a tight space, there is no room for the eye to relax. People won't read crowded text.

When text "has room to breathe," it is more inviting. This sign has more open space on its margins and between its lines.

Graphics

Graphics on interpretive signs convey detailed stories in concise and dramatic ways. A single graphic image can replace many words. They can also focus attention and lead the eye through a message sequence. Graphics also add beauty and interest to a sign face. Graphic images have more impact than words.

For more information about using images to effectively tell your message, see Chapter 4: The Message.

Miami Metro Zoo, Florida

The large graphic of a crocodile on this back-lit sign draws attention. The illustration reveals specific adaptations that may be difficult to see on the actual animal.

Auckland, New Zealand

Visitors to this New Zealand park can quickly identify the activities that are and are not allowed.

Boulder, Colorado

Without reading a word, this illustration vividly contrasts the different nocturnal hunting methods of owls and bats.

Universal Symbols

Communicate through the universal language of symbols. Symbols and objects are more identifiable than words. Even a young child can recognize the "Golden Arches" of a McDonald's restaurant or the familiar face of Smokey Bear.

Visual images may be the best way to communicate with non-reading or international visitors.

A large segment of our population cannot read and we need to accommodate them.

Federal agencies use a standardized set of recreational symbols, approved by a Federal Interagency Committee in 1983. Some of these symbols are listed below.

Cumberland Island National Seashore, Georgia

General

Area where deer might be viewed by visitors.

A light house.

Visitor information.

Drinking water.

Recreation

Cross-country ski trail.

Interpretive trail.

Hiking trail.

Area where swimming permitted.

Accommodations or Service

Area where public camping permitted.

Restrooms for men and women.

Picnic shelter.

Area where campfires permitted.

For a complete set of symbols, refer to Code of Federal Regulations, Parks, Forests, and Public Property, *Volume 36, Part 1.10, "Symbolic Signs."*

Design Fundamentals

Design is the organization of the visual elements of a sign. Every good sign has a focal point, movement, balance, unity, and proportion in varying degrees. Design can be largely intuitive, but a pleasing visual image follows certain principles.

Focal Points and Visual Flow

Plan for a strong **focal point** or center of interest that visitors will look at first. Then use varying levels of graphics and text to lead visitors through a **visual sequence**. This logo leads the eye clockwise through the title and symbols of the park.

Sea Life Park, California

Planned visual flow

When a circular logo serves as a focal point, a "break," such as this small soaring hawk, can lead the eye out of the circle and into a title. Without a break, the eye continues to circle the logo.

Planned visual flow

Schmeeckle Reserve, Wisconsin

Uinta National Forest, Utah

In addition to graphics, letter sizes dictate the eyes' direction of travel. Larger letters are read first.

Planned visual flow

People and animals on signs should usually be moving into or looking toward the text.

Notice that the moose antler connects with the title. Breaking lines create eye focusing tension. The moose captures the eye and the antlers lead into the title.

Glacier National Park, Montana

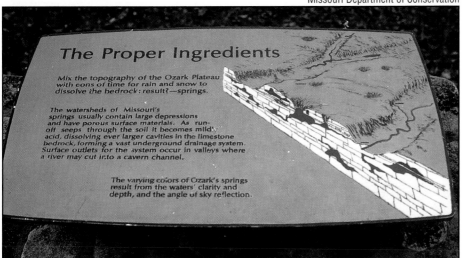

Planned visual flow

The eye is led by the converging lines of this illustration and title.

Missouri Department of Conservation

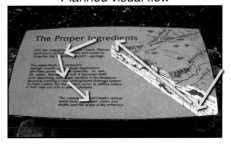

Planned visual flow

Balance and Unity

Use asymmetry for a higher Fraction of Selection.

Squares or combinations of squares should be avoided. This panel has been divided into thirds and mounted asymmetrically to add visual interest. Visual divisions into thirds are preferable to halves. Formal symmetry is balanced and at rest. Asymmetry is dynamic.

Acadia National Park, Maine

Avoid using equal spaces.

Panel faces arranged in halves are less appealing. Neither side of the panel demands your attention. Larger headings and a hierarchy of text and graphic sizes would provoke more interest. If both spaces are equal, it implies everything is equally important, with no focal point.

Aransas National Wildlife Refuge, Texas

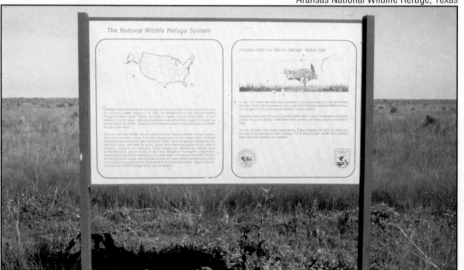

Use borders to group sign elements.

Borders, or in this case a rope, can frame and unify loose elements of a sign face. The maritime motif connects the sign and the site.

Whitefish Point Lighthouse, Michigan

Lines

Vertical lines imply power. Vertical supports blend with a forest environment.

Gray's Lake National Wildlife Refuge, Idaho

Horizontal lines generally convey peacefulness. Long low signs fit well in a marsh setting.

An overlook at the end of a short climb provides visitors with information on whooping cranes and a spotting scope to assist in viewing birds.

Color

Color provides variety, emphasis, and unity along with the illusion of depth. It can evoke a mood and complement the theme or landscape.

Schmeeckle Reserve, Wisconsin

Schmeeckle Reserve, Wisconsin

Glacier National Park, Montana

The bright background in this logo captures a visitor's attention. The yellow border unifies the elements. Yellow letters on a brown background create contrast and emphasis.

These bright yellow and orange letters are exciting and active, fitting the trail's purpose. Warm letters on a dark background "advance" toward a viewer, giving a three-dimensional quality to the sign.

This strong color contrast emphasizes the message.

Mount Rushmore National Memorial, South Dakota

The use of "red, white, and blue" reinforces the patriotic American theme at Mount Rushmore National Memorial.

Mount St. Helens National Volcanic Monument, Washington

The mood of this sign is introverted and passive. Value contrasts are minimal, gray predominates, and the opposing maroon lettering is relatively neutral. It effectively complements the somber landscape.

Schmeeckle Reserve, Wisconsin

A splash of color on a neutral background commands attention.

Schmeeckle Reserve, Wisconsin

Sometimes the natural beauty of wood and a small amount of color is the most appropriate signage for a wild area.

Blue Springs State Park, Florida

Light-colored backgrounds with dark letters are more readable in shaded areas.

Badlands National Park, South Dakota

Dark signs with light letters are easier to read in bright sun.

Design Checklist

To increase the Fraction of Selection:

• Keep the sign face simple and uncluttered.

• Maintain open space, especially on margins.

• Have a strong center of interest or focal point.

• Develop a visual sequence from the focal point. Do this through graphics and varying message levels.

• Connect all signs to each other and to their environment.

• Create short and readable messages.

• Choose readable typefaces.

• Use a minimum of CAPITAL letters.

• Use symbols and graphics, not just words.

Unifying Signage

Unity is the key to an effective signage plan. A "family" of signs can be developed by replicating design elements, such as title bars, font styles, text sizes, and colors. Using the same materials for the panels and bases is also important.

Every trail, byway, or distinct area should have a standardized sign format. However, don't be limited by the format. Find creative and new ways to tell your story within the framework.

Unified signage creates an identify for your site in the eyes of visitors.

Newberry National Volcanic Monument, Oregon

Wayside exhibits along the Big Obsidian Flow interpretive trail are creatively unified. The title font and obsidian graphic are replicated. All panels share similar colorful illustrations over a white background. The bases are constructed from obsidian rock.

This family of signs along the Logan Canyon Scenic Byway share many elements: rust colored title bars, textured sidebars with the main message, byway symbols in the upper left, large historic photographs and illustrations, gray backgrounds, stylized title fonts, and sans serif message fonts.

Logan Canyon National Scenic Byway, Utah

USS Arizona National Memorial, Hawaii

Saguaro National Park, Arizona

The National Park Service's **Unigrid System** is a standardized graphics template that unifies wayside exhibits, signs, and publications in every national park and monument. The black title bar and white sans serif title are synonymous with National Park Service interpretation.

Find ways of "breaking the grid" when working with standardized layouts. The Unigrid System allows for flexibility and creativity. The cactus overlapping the title bar creates a focal point and is more interesting to visitors.

Universal Design

Signs and wayside exhibits should be accessible to the widest range of visitors possible. Universal design celebrates the fact that there is no "average person." Each of us is a distinct individual with our own learning style, personality, and physical ability. Universally accessible signs require:

- **Physical access.** Signs that allow everyone to hear, touch, see, and do.
- **Program access.** Signs that have no communication barriers. Messages should be provided in a variety of ways: graphics, text, audio, tactile, interactive and participatory devices. Messages should also be free of cultural and ethnic bias and be communicated in simple language easily understood by all.

Accessibility Guidelines for Wayside Exhibits

These National Park Service guidelines were developed by Harpers Ferry Center, Division of Wayside Exhibits. Wayside exhibits should be accessible to all visitors.

Visitors Who are Mobility Impaired

- Wayside exhibits will be installed at accessible locations wherever possible.
- Wayside exhibit panels will be installed at heights and angles favorable for viewing by most visitors, including those is wheelchairs. For standard NPS low-profile units, the recommended height is 30-34" from the bottom of the exhibit panel to finished grade; for vertical exhibits and bulletin boards the height is 24-28", depending on panel size.
- Trailhead exhibits will include accessibility advisory.
- Wayside exhibits will have level, hard-surfaced exhibit pads.
- Exhibit sites will offer clean, unrestricted views of park features described in exhibits.

Visitors Who are Visually Impaired

- Exhibit type will be as legible and readable as possible.
- Panel colors will be selected to reduce eye strain and glare, and to provide excellent readability under field conditions. White should not be used for a background color.
- Selected wayside exhibits may incorporate audio stations or tactile elements such as models, texture blocks, and relief maps.
- For all major features interpreted by graphic wayside exhibits, the park should offer non-visual interpretation covering the same subject matter. Examples include audio tours, radio messages, and ranger talks.
- Use the table on page 34 for letter sizes for the visually impaired.

Visitors Who are Hearing Impaired

- Wayside exhibit panels will communicate visually, and will rely heavily on graphics to interpret park resources.
- Essential information included in audio station messages will be duplicated in written form, either as part of the exhibit text or in a publication.

Visitors Who have Learning Disabilities

- Topics for wayside exhibits will be specific and of general interest. Unnecessary complexity will be avoided.
- Wherever possible, easy-to-understand graphics will be used to convey ideas rather than text alone.
- Unfamiliar expressions, technical terms, and jargon will be avoided. Pronunciation aids and definitions will be provided where needed.
- Text will be concise and free of long paragraphs and wordy language.

Chapter 4:
The Message

In 1821, the United States assumed control of Flori[da]
federal troops occupied the fort. It was renamed Ft.
for the Revolutionary war hero Francis Marion, the
"Swamp Fox."

In order to modernize the fort's defense[...]
of the moat was filled in and modern en[...]
The middle structure in the moat is a f[...]
used for heating cannon balls, a hea[...]

Ft. Marion remained an a[...]

Except for the rare instances of in-spiration, I should guess that the adequate interpretive inscription will be the result of ninety percent thinking and ten percent compo-sition. Inspiration is usually the mirrored reflection of hard work.

Freeman Tilden
Interpreting Our Heritage

Castillo de San Marcos National Monument, Florida

Developing an Effective Message

Interpretive signs compete for the visitor's attention with warm sunshine, cold rains, and colorful birds. They are static objects in a dynamic environment.

To be effective, an interpretive sign must communicate quickly and dramatically. The message must be important to the visitor and relate to what they can see or experience.

The visitor must feel that reading this sign is worth the effort. Too much work for no apparent reward means the message will be ignored.

By following some simple steps, you can help visitors access and find meaning in the interpretive stories of your site and resources.

Ice Age National Scenic Trail, Wisconsin

Seven Ways to an Effective Message

1. **Say it visually.** Use photos and drawings to help tell the story.

2. **Graphics should do more than duplicate what can be seen.** They should reveal hidden meanings and ideas.

3. **Use a message pyramid.** Develop a descending order of message importance. This can be expressed as the **3-30-3 rule**. Visitors can receive a message in three seconds, thirty seconds, or three minutes.

4. **Keep the message short.** Use short sentences and paragraphs. Use a readability scale such as the Flesch test to help eliminate wordy phrases and paragraphs.

5. Create imagery with **concrete nouns and active verbs.** Limit adjectives and adverbs.

6. **Relate to the visitor's experience.** Use personal pronouns, personal language, and familiar terms. Illustrate with metaphors, analogies, quotes, and real examples.

7. **Provide for multi-sensory involvement.** Use digital audio repeaters and participatory devices. These may include tactiles, models, relief maps, flip panels, and interactives.

Say it Visually

"A picture is worth a thousand words."

This cliché is especially true of signs. Visitors avoid panels with too much text. Illustrations and photographs tell the story in concise and intriguing ways, often better than narratives.

Great Blue Heron behaviors are illustrated on this sign. The visual representations are easier to understand than the text descriptions.

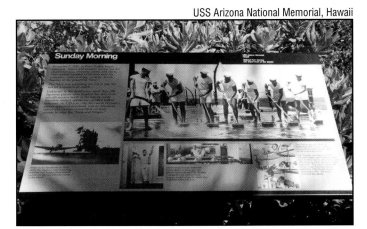

Photographs help bring historic events to life. Pictures of people are especially powerful.

Graphics show events that cannot be directly experienced, like a blazing prairie fire.

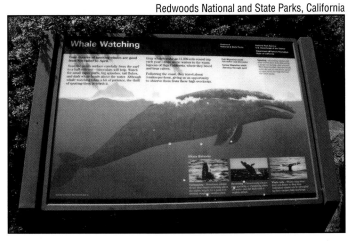

Use large focal point graphics to attract attention and create a visual flow. Captions have the greatest impact when they are proximal to the visuals.

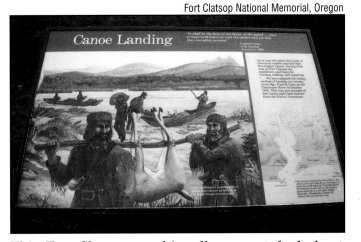

This Fort Clatsop graphic tells a great deal about the Lewis and Clark expedition without words: the types of clothing worn, animals hunted, canoes and tools used, and the historic landscape.

Graphics should do more than duplicate what can be seen.

Photographs and illustrations should reveal hidden meanings and ideas that are not immediately recognized by the visitor. Avoid adding images that replicate the landscape or resource. Use the resource as a foundation, and incorporate visuals that best tell the intriguing stories.

Little Bighorn Battlefield, Montana

Badlands National Park, South Dakota

This panel shows the bands of substrate soils in the Badlands, where specific fossils are found.

The colors and background of this panel at Little Bighorn Battlefield are nearly identical to the real landscape. The addition of calvary and warriors, however, transport visitors to the historic battle.

Arches National Park, Utah

Rogue River National Forest, Oregon

Although duplicating the landscape is usually not recommended, it can be an effective technique for labeling landforms or mountain peaks.

A cross-section of an underground lava tube illustrates how this natural bridge was formed.

Use a message pyramid.

Most visitors will look at an interpretive panel for only a few seconds. If they connect to something, they will stay longer. Well planned signs use a message pyramid or hierarchy to tell the interpretive story in different levels.

Crater Lake National Park, Oregon

30-second
message

3-second
message

3-minute
message

3-30-3 Rule

The 3-30-3 Rule is an effective method for designing signs that have a message hierarchy.

3 seconds

Most visitors will look at a sign for at least 3 seconds. This message usually includes an intriguing title and large graphics.

30 seconds

Some visitors who are interested will continue to look at a sign for about 30 seconds. The main message is usually in larger letters, and about 1 to 2 paragraphs long.

3 minutes

A few visitors who are interested in the topic will look at a sign for up to 3 minutes. More detailed information and graphics, usually of smaller size, can be provided for this group.

30-second
message

3-second
message

Denver Zoo, Colorado

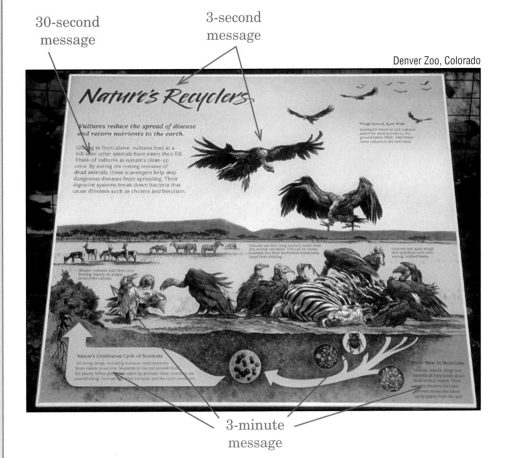

3-minute
message

Keep the message short.

"I have made this letter longer, because I have not had the time to make it shorter."

Blaise Pascal
Letters provinciales, 1657

Effective messages are short and direct. However, writing concise text is a time-consuming process that requires pruning and rewording. Simple words, concise sentences, and short paragraphs make a message more readable.

Readability tests can help keep our writing at an easy reading level. If you use a word processor, you can run several quick readability checks. Microsoft Word, for example, has the Flesch Reading Ease and Flesch-Kincaid Grade Level tests built in.

Salinas Pueblo Missions National Monument, New Mexico

"For 17th-century Catholics, this church nave was the spiritual heart of Mission San Gregorio de Abo. When worshippers—both Indian and nearby settlers from Spain—came to hear mass, they stood and knelt. There were no pews. Prayers and sacred songs echoed off these walls. At the alter ahead, the priest chanted the familiar liturgy of the Mass in Latin, the same as in any Roman Catholic church in Europe, Asia, Africa, or the Americas in those years.

"Note the outline of stones on the ground ahead. They indicate the smaller size of this church in the 1620s. Construction twenty years later left Abo's sanctuary more as you see it now, with new walls reaching 50 feet high."

Flesch Reading Ease: 66.5, Standard
Flesch-Kincaid Grade Level: 7.6, 7th-8th grade
Write Formula: 79, Average American Reader

The Write Formula

1. Count a 100 word sample

2. Count all one-syllable words except "the," "is," "are," "was," and "were." Count <u>1 point</u> for each one-syllable word.

3. Count the number of sentences in the 100-word sample to the nearest period or semicolon and give <u>3 points</u> for each sentence.

4. Add together the one-syllable word count and the three points for each sentence to get the score.

If your sign has less than 100 words, multiply your tally to get the equivalent of 100.

Score	Reading Ease
85-100+	Children's Publications
75-85	Average American Reader
65-75	Above Average American

* A score of 80 is close to ideal.

From Exhibits for the Small Museum, A Handbook,
by Arminta Neal, 1976.

Flesch Reading Ease

1. Count the number of syllables in a 100 word sample (S).

2. Calculate the average number of words per sentence in the sample (W).

3. Calculate R = 206.835 - 0.846S - 1.015W.

4. Compare value to table:

Score	Reading Ease
90-100	Very easy
80-90	Easy
70-80	Fairly easy
60-70	Standard
50-60	Fairly difficult
30-50	Difficult
0-30	Very difficult

The score can also be converted into a U.S. grade level with this formula: G = 0.39W + .118S - 15.59

From The Art of Readable Writing *by Robert Flesch, 1949.*

Use concrete nouns and active verbs.

"When you catch an adjective, kill it. No, I don't mean utterly, but kill most of them—then the rest will be valuable."

Mark Twain
Letter to D.W. Bowser, 1880

Writing concisely is more than just limiting your words; it is using the *right* words. Active language is more interesting to read and can describe a resource, site, process, or idea in less words. The temptation is to add many descriptors before a noun or verb. Choosing a concrete noun or active verb is more direct and concise.

Petroglyph National Monument, New Mexico

Badlands National Park, South Dakota

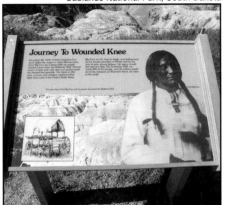

"...Serpents, spirit masks, and human-like figures stare mutely from the blackened boulders along a simple dirt trail.

"Footprints in stone beckon the spiritual explorer. Sights and sounds of the city fall away with every step farther into the canyon..."

Concrete nouns and active verbs vividly interpret stories on these panels.

"...A bitter Christmas Eve wind rattled the wagon in which Minneconjou Chief Big Foot lay waiting while his people cleared a pass down the Badlands Wall. Several hours of hard work with axes and spades made the disused trail passable."

"...His agony would last only five days. On December 29th, he, nearly 200 of his people, and 30 soldiers would die in the massacre at Wounded Knee..."

Concrete Nouns

A concrete noun describes a thing or place. Choosing the most descriptive noun can eliminate the need for adjectives.

Consider this sentence:
"The gray squirrel lives in a <u>hole</u> in a tree formed by rotting, insects, or other animals."

Use a concrete noun to make it more concise:
"The gray squirrel lives in a tree <u>den</u>."

What other synonyms describe the noun "hole" better?
Recess, groove, depression, cavity, pit, pocket, cup, cave burrow, hollow, well, notch, abyss

Active Verbs

An active verb describes an action. Choosing the most descriptive verb can eliminate the need for adverbs.

Consider this sentence:
"The butterfly <u>flapped</u> its wings and <u>flew erratically</u> from flower to flower."

Use an active verb to make it more concise:
"The butterfly <u>fluttered</u> from flower to flower."

What other active verb synonyms describe "fly" more effectively?
Soar, glide, dive, flap, dart, float, skim, scud, shoot, sail, buzz, hover, cruise, waft, dart, flit

Relate to the visitor's experience.

If a story is to mean something to a visitor, it must relate to something within that person's experience. Use personal pronouns, personal language, and familiar terms to make your wayside exhibits more friendly and inviting.

Glencoe, Scotland

Personal Pronouns and Language

Write like you are having a conversation with the visitor:
- Use words like "you," "your," "we," "our," "us," "I," and "me."
- Use narratives, questions, requests, and command sentences.

Consider this panel text:
"Visitors to Pine Glen use hundreds of gallons of water every day. The water comes from the large reservoir one can see below this sign."

Rewrite it more personally:
"How much water have you used today? Look at the large lake below you. Hundreds of gallons are pumped from this reservoir every day for Pine Glen visitors, like you."

Familiar Terms

Panels with complex words or technical ideas are usually ignored.
- Do not use technical jargon. If an unfamiliar term must be used, it should have a simple definition.
- Avoid using clichés. Although personal, overused clichés can detract from the primary message.

"Hello! I am the innkeeper Donald McInnes. I was encouraged to take on the Kingshouse in the early 1770's after a distinguished career in King George's army. But making a living here has proved a lot more difficult than I had been led to believe!

"...I should not be telling you this, but recently I have had to resort to the illegal trade in whisky and salt. How else can a man make a living in this God-forsaken place?"

Newberry National Volcanic Monument, Oregon

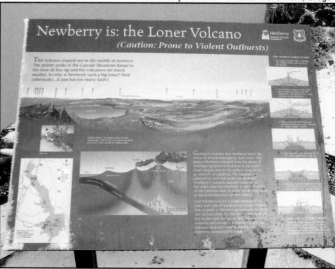

"This volcano erupted out in the middle of nowhere. The pointy peaks of the Cascade Mountain Range to the west all line up and the volcanoes are much smaller. So why is Newberry such a big loner? Well (obviously)...it just has too many faults!"

The goal of a message is to connect visitors to the meanings of a resource. The use of creative tools, like comparisons, quotes, and real examples, help make these connections stronger and relate better to our audience.

Metaphors and Similes

Compare a resource with something common to the visitor's experience.

"The layers of a forest are like different stories in a wildlife apartment building."

Analogies

Compare the relationship between two items, and apply that relationship to the resource.

"Like a person with a parachute drifting in the wind, a milkweed seed is carried far from its mother plant."

Quotes and Real Examples

Quotes are powerful because they are written thoughts and feelings of someone associated with a site or an event.

Other real examples include scientific research, news articles, stories from the site, and local legends. These help enhance the sense of place.

Glacier National Park, Montana

This visual metaphor compares the glacier to a conveyor belt.

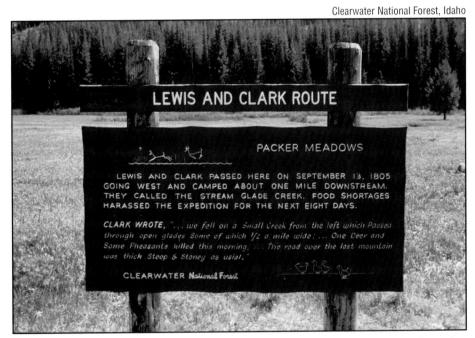

Clearwater National Forest, Idaho

A real quote from Clark's journal helps to connect visitors to this significant place.

Provide for multi-sensory involvement.

Adding participatory components to a wayside exhibit can help tell your story in a unique and engaging way. Audio units, tactiles, flip panels, and other devices encourage the use of different senses, while physically involving the visitor.

When deciding whether or not to add a multi-sensory component to your sign, consider the following:

- **Will the experience be enhanced by this component?** Be sure the device will help to tell the story.

- **What is the vandalism potential at my site?** Multi-sensory components are often more vandal-prone.

- **What is my budget?** Durable components can add significant cost to each sign.

Tactile Exhibits

A tactile exhibit encourages visitor involvement. Attaching models, casts, or bas-reliefs to a sign attracts attention, enhances learning by providing a three-dimensional experience, and offers an additional opportunity for interaction. Studies show that three-dimensional elements increase a sign panel's attraction and holding power.

Corkscrew Swamp Audubon Sanctuary, Florida

Protecting the Plume Birds

Hunted almost to extinction for their feathers

San Antonio Missions National Historic Park, Texas

Three-dimensional models help visitors see and feel a site from a different perspective.

Crowley's Ridge Nature Center, Arkansas

Bas-relief model of a butterfly life cycle.

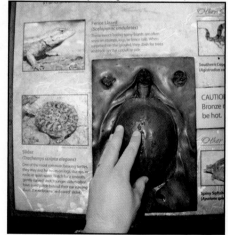
Crowley's Ridge Nature Center, Arkansas

Bronze model of a turtle swimming.

Audio Exhibits

An audio message requires no reading, communicates more information than signs, and is easily changed. Human voices and sound effects help connect visitors on an emotional level.

Lorance Creek State Natural Area, Arkansas

Beinn Eighe National Nature Reserve, Scotland

An exhibit at Lorance Creek State Natural Area in Arkansas plays the call of a treefrog.

The audio unit is powered by a solar panel in the canopy. The power supply and speaker are hidden high up a tree trunk inside a camouflaged box.

As an alternative to push buttons, visitors to Beinn Eighe National Nature Reserve in Scotland spin a wheel to hear the audio message. This powers the unit, while providing the message in two languages depending on which way the crank is turned.

Production Tips for Audio Messages

- Keep it short. Three minutes or less is optimal in most situations.

- A production should always sound live rather than canned. Don't sound like you are reading from a script. Use the first person and second person where possible.

- Pretest your scripts for pacing and comprehension before recording.

- Use sound effects. Natural sounds and background effects set a mood for the message.

- Use voices in dialect. When used appropriately, they transport the visitor back in time and place.

- Use professional production studios, but make your interpretive themes and wishes clear to them. Local radio stations and private studios can help you produce high quality recorded messages.

- Use digital sound equipment to ensure durability.

- Provide important information in text form for visitors who may have difficulty hearing.

Interactive Exhibits

Flip panels, viewing tubes, mounted objects and artifacts, and other tactile components encourage visitors to physically discover different stories. Nearly any device can be incorporated into a wayside exhibit. Your imagination and budget are the only limitations.

Science Museum of Minnesota, Minnesota

Real objects can have powerful connections to the resource. These jars are filled with different types of cargo that barges haul.

Capilano Suspension Bridge, Canada

Spinning the wheel causes the owl to move its eyes.

Sandia Peak, New Mexico

Viewing tubes focus attention on features of the landscape.

Battleship Missouri Memorial, Hawaii

Each wayside exhibit on this battleship features a different symbol that can be stamped into a "passport."

Visitors flip up a simulated rock on this panel to see the creatures that live in a stream.

Golden Gate Canyon State Park, Colorado

Knockan Crag National Nature Reserve, Scotland

Knockan Crag National Nature Reserve in Scotland is an important geologic site. Here, studies of the rock formations eventually led to the understanding of plate tectonics.

All of the exhibits are creatively and artistically designed around this central theme. Interactive components encourage visitors to be engaged in the total experience.

An open-air kiosk blends into the hillside and encourages exploration. The roof protects a series of elaborate interactive exhibits.

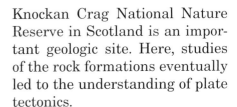

On the site, sculpted hands invite you to touch both the old and new layers of rock.

Improving Messages

Example 1 - Original Sign and Message

MANY PARKS CURVE

THE IMPRINT OF ICE. MUCH OF THE SURROUNDING SCENERY WAS SHAPED BY GLACIAL ICE OVER 15,000 YEARS AGO. DURING THAT TIME THE COLD CLIMATE ALLOWED GLACIERS TO FORM IN MOUNTAIN RECESSES HIGH ABOVE. EVENTUALLY, ALL OF THE MAJOR CANYONS IN AND AROUND ROCKY MOUNTAIN NATIONAL PARK WERE FILLED WITH TONS OF ICE, SOME TO A DEPTH OF 1,500 FEET. AS THESE FROZEN TRIBUTARIES DESCENDED TO LOWER ELEVATIONS, THEY SCOURED AND POLISHED THE LANDSCAPE, CREATING THE STRIATED SLOPES AND U-SHAPED CANYONS.

IN THE VALLEYS BELOW, GLACIERS FORMED A MASSIVE PLUG 200 FEET THICK AND MORE THAN EIGHT MILES LONG. THESE ICY GIANTS DOMINATED THE SCENE UNTIL APPROXIMATELY 13,000 TO 14,000 YEARS AGO, WHEN A WARMING CLIMATE CAUSED THE GLACIERS TO BEGIN THEIR RETREAT. VAST QUANTITIES OF DEBRIS RELEASED BY MELTING ICE FORMED HUGE MOUNDS CALLED MORAINES. IN MORAINE PARK, THESE FEATURES APPEAR AS LONG, TREE-COVERED RIDGES.

THOUGH THE ANCIENT GLACIERS HAVE LONG SINCE WASTED AWAY, IMPRINTS OF THEIR PASSING REMAIN AS SOME OF THE MOST SPECTACULAR SCENERY IN NORTH AMERICA.

ABOUT GLACIERS. GLACIERS BEGIN AS SNOW FIELDS HIGH ABOVE THE THAW LINE. AS THESE SNOW FIELDS BECOME DEEPER, THEY COMPACT INTO GRANULAR MASSES OF ICE. GRADUALLY THESE FIELDS THICKEN UNTIL THEIR OWN INTERNAL WEIGHT, COMBINED WITH GRAVITY, CAUSES THEM TO FLOW AS GLACIERS.

GLACIERS SHAPED THE LANDSCAPE BY PLUCKING, SHEARING, AND COMPRESSING AS THEY MOVE. MOVEMENT INSIDE THE ICE MASS IS ALWAYS FORWARD, SO THE COLLECTED DEBRIS IS ALWAYS VARIED TOWARD THE FRONT, ADDING TO THE GLACIER'S ABRASIVE POWER.

THOUGH GLACIERS MAY LAST FOR THOUSANDS OF YEARS, THE ICE MAY BE ONLY HUNDREDS OF YEARS OLD. THE ICE, CONSTANTLY BEING REPLENISHED FROM ABOVE, LASTS AS LONG AS IT TAKES TO MOVE FROM THE CIRQUE TO THE FRONT OF THE GLACIER. IT CRAWLS FROM SEVERAL INCHES TO SEVERAL FEET PER DAY.

WHEN GLACIERS RECEDE FASTER THAN THEY ADVANCE, THEY RELEASE A VAST AMOUNT OF ROCK, SAND, AND OTHER DEBRIS WHICH WAS PICKED UP ALONG THE WAY. WHEN LEFT IN ELONGATED PILES, THIS MATERIAL FORMS THE LATERAL AND END MORAINES, THE LATTER MARKING THE FARTHEST POINT REACHED BY THE ICE FIELD.

Recommendations for Change

Implied Purpose:
To illustrate to the visitor how glaciers changed the landscape.

Recommendations:
- Shorten and simplify message.
- Use vivid language.
- Create a message pyramid.
- Change capital letters to lower case.
- Set text ragged right.
- Move text over graphic illustrations.

(revised text)   The Imprint of Ice

Glaciers carved these mountains and valleys more than 15,000 years ago.

Snow accumulated in high, shaded valleys until it was compressed into flowing ice. Glaciers surged to life, bulldozing and scouring the valleys.

Warmer summers shrank the glaciers back to the high snowfields we see today.

Bowl-shaped depressions, called cirques, mark places where glaciers are born.

U-shaped valleys are remnants of a glacier's passage.

Moraines are lines of debris dropped when the glaciers melted.

Look for evidence of these extinct glaciers as you tour the Rockies.

New Reading Ease Score = 73, Fairly Easy

Redesign courtesy of Wilderness Graphics, Inc.

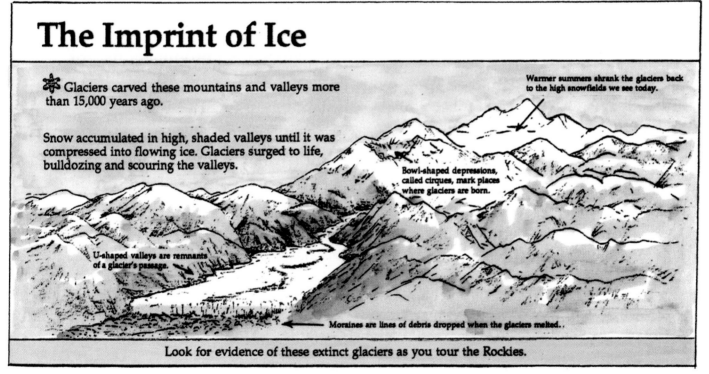

Example 2 - Original Sign and Message

Freshwater Marsh

The natural values of freshwater marshes have just begun to be understood. An obvious value is their importance to wildlife. The nightly chorus of frogs and toads reflect their abundance. Salamanders congregate to lay eggs. Newly spawned sunfish, bass, and bullheads hide among the reeds and cattails. Marshes provide important habitat for migrating birds, as well as deer, raccoon, bobcat, muskrat, and mink.

Alligators are a prominent part of the wildlife in these marshes. Alligators often dig large holes which serve as reservoirs during dry periods. Thus "gator" holes provide the source for renewal of life when the marsh is flooded again.

Freshwater marshes provide floodwater storage, wastewater storage, and groundwater recharging. They are, indeed, a most valuable part of our natural resources.

Recommendations for Change

Implied Purpose:
To communicate the value and diversity of a freshwater marsh.

Recommendations:
- Write message for someone who is sitting in a car, on-site.
- Shorten and simplify message.
- Use vivid language.
- Create a message pyramid.
- Use a graphic that simplifies and organizes the message.

(revised text)   **Reservoirs of Life**

This marsh is a living sponge. It filters and purifies water. It is home to a diverse abundance of plants and animals.

What Does a Marsh Do for You?
The marsh stores water and slowly releases it to the groundwater. Marsh plants filter pollutants from your drinking water. They protect from floods by slowing the runoff of rainwater. Marshes are truly reservoirs of life for all creatures, including us.

Gator Holes
During dry seasons, depressions dug by "gators" store water. Many creatures survive drought in these dangerous "refuges." A few will be eaten by the resident gator.

New Reading Ease Score = 70, Fairly Easy

Redesign courtesy of Wilderness Graphics, Inc.

Example 3 - Original Sign and Message

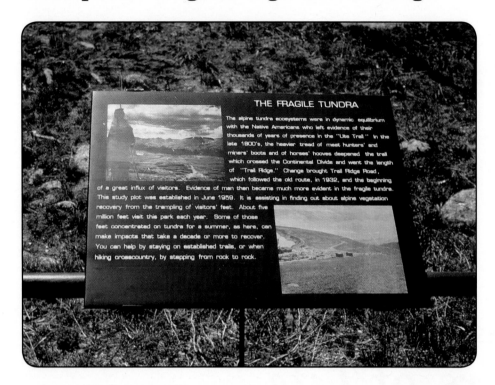

THE FRAGILE TUNDRA

The alpine tundra ecosystems were in dynamic equilibrium with the Native Americans who left evidence of their thousands of years of presence in the "Ute Trail." In the late 1800's, the heavier tread of meat hunters' and miners' boots and of horses' hooves deepened the trail which crossed the continental divide and went the length of "Trail Ridge." Change brought Trail Ridge Road, which followed the old route, in 1932, and the beginning of a great influx of visitors. Evidence of man then became much more evident in the fragile tundra. This study plot was established in June 1959. It is assisting in finding out about alpine vegetation recovery from the trampling of visitor's feet. About five million feet visit the park each year. Some of those feet concentrated on tundra for a summer, as here, can make impacts that can take a decade or more to recover. You can help by staying on established trails, or when hiking crosscountry, by stepping from rock to rock.

Recommendations for Change

Implied Purpose:
To demonstrate to visitors the effect they have on the tundra.

Recommendations:
- Create a message pyramid.
- Simplify and shorten message.
- Reduce length of sentences.
- Use vivid, active language.
- Replace photos with line drawings to better illustrate the message and to create a visual flow.
- Reset type to more readable line length and layout.

(revised text)   The Trampled Tundra

This plot has been protected since 1959. It is testimony to the slow recovery of the tundra from the trample of human feet.

The occasional moccasin on the old Ute Trail had little impact. In the 1800's, boots of miners and hunters and the hooves of their horses cut the tundra into ribbons of trails. Trail Ridge Road opened in 1932 to caravans of tourists. Five million feet now visit the park each year.

Help heal the tundra. Stay on marked trails or step from rock to rock when hiking cross-country.

New Reading Ease Score: 79, Fairly Easy

Redesign courtesy of Wilderness Graphics, Inc.

Beyond Prose

Like poetry and paintings, a sign message should inspire and provoke in bold and simple languages. It is an art form of the essence. The quantity of words is often inversely proportional to the success of a sign. Strive for fresh perspectives, poetic twists, vivid imagery, and simple eloquence.

The challenge of the inscription writer is to involve the reader intellectually, emotionally, or physically. The message should help the visitor see the site in new and meaningful ways.

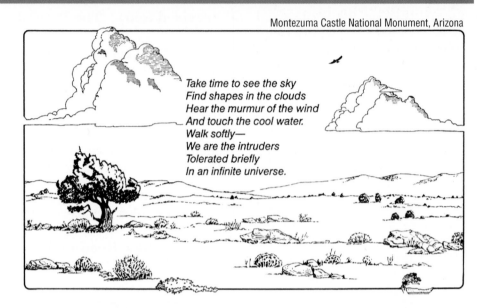

Montezuma Castle National Monument, Arizona

Take time to see the sky
Find shapes in the clouds
Hear the murmur of the wind
And touch the cool water.
Walk softly—
We are the intruders
Tolerated briefly
In an infinite universe.

A sign like this one greeted wilderness campers at the Philmont Scout Ranch in the 1960s. Detailed explanation is not always effective communication. "Monument to a Careless Camper" actively provokes the reader to ponder meaning beyond the words.

MONUMENT TO A CARELESS CAMPER

Industrial forest site, Wisconsin

FORESTRY AT WORK

In 1974, a sleet storm devastated over 7,000 acres of Nekoosa's timberland. Salvage of this 155 acre setting was accomplished the following year and 2,300 cords of pulpwood were harvested. That would provide 460,000 reams of fine writing and printing paper for market.

Following the harvest, the setting was prepared for planting by churning up the land with large tractors pulling discs. This left a relatively clean seedbed for planting the next crop. Each acre was then planted with 900 carefully selected Norway red pine from Nekoosa's own nursery—a total of 139,500 trees. Some of these will be harvested during the growing cycle to give the remaining trees more room to grow, more sunlight and nutrients. For comparison look at the untreated area to the left and right of the platform.

When the final stand harvest is conducted, around the year 2020, this site will have produced approximately 50 cords of fine raw material per acre—about 35 more cords per acre than was produced by the less intensively managed natural forest—enough raw material to provide 1,550,000 reams of fine writing and printing paper.

Your forest industry using intensive management provides all of us with a habitat for wildlife and a place for recreation.

TREES ARE AMERICA'S RENEWABLE RESOURCE.

Both of these forest industry waysides have the same purpose. They explain forest management practices, often a public relations problem. Which message do you feel is most successfully communicated?

The simple understatement of the Rayonier sign promises that the forest will be renewed.

Industrial forest site, Olympic Peninsula, Washington

Chapter 5:
Sign Fabrication and Installation

Schmeeckle Reserve, Wisconsin

When asked, visitors to natural areas say they prefer to see few, if any, signs. They are seeking an experience in a pristine environment. Signs are considered an intrusion.

Signs must strike a balance between meeting a visitor's need for information and keeping the site natural. Rustic, routed wood is often the best choice for natural areas. Anodized aluminum may be better suited to historical or cultural sites. A zoo may require the vivid colors of porcelain enamel or high pressure laminate.

Technical skill alone is not enough to create good signs. There must be harmony between materials, design, and the site. This requires insight and a well-developed sense of aesthetics. Someone with sensitivity to all aspects of the project should work with fabricators throughout the process.

The technologies and tools for fabricating signs are virtually unlimited. Many companies specialize in one or more aspects of sign fabrication. See the Resources section for listings of companies that might help you with your project.

Sign Panels

Sign panels can be created from many materials including metal, fiberglass, wood, concrete, and plastic. These materials can be made attractive and vibrant by variations of color, illumination, texture, and shape. **Durability, aesthetics, and cost** are the main criteria for panel selection.

High Pressure Laminate

Taylor Creek Visitor Center, Nevada

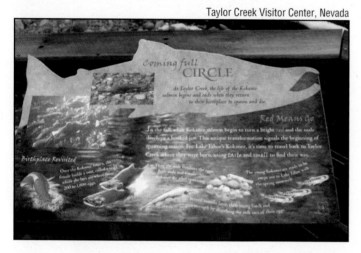

High pressure laminate signs are a cost effective means of producing vividly colored and detailed interpretive messages. The material is produced in the same way as a kitchen countertop. Introduced in the mid-1990s, it quickly became one of the most popular options for interpretive signs.

Fabrication Process:
1. A digital file is printed onto a special sheet of paper impregnated with melamine resins. Melamine is a harmless type of plastic that cannot be melted or reshaped after being molded once.
2. A UV-resistant overlaminate is placed over the print. Several layers of phenolic resin sheets (another type of plastic) are placed below the print. More layers make the sign thicker.
3. The layers are pressed at high heat and pressure for an extended period of time. The entire assembly is fused into a single plastic panel.

Best Uses:
Where detailed, full-color graphics are needed, such as wayside exhibits and trail panels.

Advantages:
- Durable. Resistant to weather and vandalism. Most companies offer a 10-20 year warranty against fading and delaminating.
- Good graphic detail
- Unlimited number of colors
- Graffiti resistant: paint and marker easily removed
- Can be produced in a variety of thicknesses: 1/2" or greater do not require framing
- Can be cut into a variety of shapes
- Low cost: $50-$70 per sq. ft.
- Fast turn-around time: 3-6 weeks

Disadvantages:
- Thin panels require framing and backing
- Can be scratched, but minor scratches can be buffed out with car wax
- Duplicates are usually same price as original
- Thicker panels do not require a frame, but are more prone to vandalism
- Not as time tested as some of the other materials

The Falkirk Wheel, Scotland

Photo courtesy of iZone: *www.izoneimaging.com*

Fiberglass Embedment

Chesapeake Bay Gateway, Virginia Living Museum, Virginia

Photo courtesy of Pannier Graphics: *www.panniergraphics.com*

Best Uses:
Where detailed, full-color graphics are needed, such as wayside exhibits and trail panels.

Advantages:
- Can embed a silk-screened or digital print
- Silk-screened prints are durable. Resistant to weather and vandalism. Most companies offer a 10 year warranty against fading and delaminating
- Good graphic detail and full color available
- Digital prints low cost: $40-$60 per sq. ft.
- Can duplicate copies of prints for a very reduced price. These can be embedded economically at a later date
- Fast turn-around time: 4-6 weeks

Disadvantages:
- Silk-screened prints high cost: $250-$530 per sq. ft. Price increases as number of colors increase
- Thin panels require framing and backing
- Digital prints moderately durable. Most companies offer a 5-10 year warranty against fading
- Can be scratched, but minor scratches can be buffed out with car wax
- Fiberglass texture is visible and can yellow over time

Fiberglass embedment is a time-tested, cost effective signage process, capable of producing full-color detailed graphics. Silk-screened prints embedded in fiberglass have been used by interpretive sites since the early 1970s. More recently, embedded digital prints save time and money, while allowing unlimited colors.

Fabrication Process:
1. A digital file is printed or a layout is silk-screened onto paper.
2. The print is laid between layers of fiberglass mat and saturated with clear, UV-resistant, polyester resin.
3. A single fused fiberglass-reinforced panel is formed with embedded subsurface graphics.

Fort Caroline National Memorial, Timucuan Preserve, Florida

After several years of harsh conditions, the fiberglass texture of this sign became more visible. New technologies are reducing this issue.

Porcelain Enamel

Porcelain enamel is a premier interpretive panel material. Its superior color and sharp graphic detail are unrivaled. The material is also the most durable, impervious to sunlight and most other natural elements.

Fabrication Process:
1. A mixture of glass particles is applied to a steel substrate.
2. One color from the layout is applied with special glass-based inks (inorganic pigments). These are either printed directly from a digital file or silk screened.
3. The mixture is fired at very high temperatures (1100°F - 1600°F). The glass and inks are fused to the steel, creating a permanent coating.
4. Another color is added and the panel is fired again. This is repeated for all colors.

George Washington Birthplace National Monument, Virginia

Crater Lake National Park, Oregon

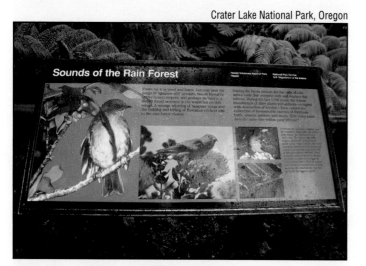

White-winged scoters and *surf scoters* can be seen in the water or in the air just above the waves. They nest in Canada and Alaska and winter along the coast as far south as Baja California.

If porcelain enamel chips, it will begin to rust from the inside.

Best Uses:
Where colorful and detailed graphics are needed as in zoos and other high use areas. Also where there is extended UV exposure, such as desert areas or high elevations.

Advantages:
- Very durable. Impervious to most natural elements. Most companies offer a 25 year warranty, but signs can last 40 years or longer.
- Excellent, high-resolution graphic detail
- Vivid colors that do not fade
- Little maintenance required
- Graffiti resistant: paint and markers easily removed
- Very resistant to scratches
- Can be cut in a variety of shapes

Disadvantages:
- High initial cost: $300-$600 per sq. ft.
- Price increases as number of colors increase
- Requires framing or backing
- If chipped, the panel will rust from the inside out, especially near oceans
- Shiny surface can cause glare in the sun
- Slower turn-around time: 10-12 weeks
- Duplicates are same price as the original

Color-Embedded Anodized Aluminum

Anodized aluminum offers another very durable material for interpretive signage. **Anodizing** is the process of inducing oxidation over the surface of aluminum, making it 60 times harder. A recently developed process allows full color to be embedded within the metal surface. The signs are impervious to sunlight and most natural elements.

Fabrication Process:
1. An aluminum oxide layer is evenly distributed across a thin aluminum sheet. The pores are opened so they can accept ink.
2. The pores are filled with dyes. Each color is applied separately.
3. Aluminum sheets are immersed in a hot acid bath to seal the pores under a layer of clear aluminum oxide crystals.

Sydney Olympic Park, Sydney, Australia

Photo courtesy of ALUimage: *www.aluimage.com*

Maroubra Beach Skate Park, New South Wales, Australia

Echo Point, Katoomba, Australia

Photos courtesy of ALUimage: *www.aluimage.com*

Best Uses:
Where colorful and durable signage is needed. Metal material works best for memorial plaques, historic sites, zoos, waysides, and other high-traffic areas.

Advantages:
- Very durable. Impervious to most natural elements. Many companies offer a 20 year warranty, but signs can last 40 years or longer.
- Will not rust and colors do not fade
- Little maintenance required
- Graffiti resistant: paint and marker are easily removed
- Panels can be cut in a variety of shapes
- Fast turn-around time: 4-6 weeks
- Duplicates less expensive than original
- Moderate cost: $100-$150 per sq. ft.

Disadvantages:
- Requires framing and backing
- Medium photograph detail
- Price increases as number of colors increase
- Graphics have a metallic shine
- White colors cannot be reproduced; bare aluminum shows through instead
- Can be scratched, but minor scratches can be buffed out with car wax
- Not as time tested as some of the other materials

Photo-Chemically Etched Anodized Aluminum

Saguaro National Monument, Arizona

Novalloy Metal Micro-Imaging
Photo courtesy of Interpretive Graphics: *www.interpretivegraphics.com*

Etched hard-coat anodized aluminum (metal micro-imaging) is a time-tested, durable material, perfect for applications not requiring full-color. The signs have been successfully used at interpretive sites since the mid-1970s. The material is impervious to sunlight and other natural elements.

Fabrication Process:

1. A 3/8"-thick aluminum plate is anodized, increasing its hardness and changing its color.
2. It is surfaced with a photo sensitive coating, exposed to intense light, and submerged in acid.
3. The acid etches images and text into its surface.
4. The sign is re-anodized, hardening and coloring the new etchings.

Best Uses:

Where full-color is not needed. Historical interpretation, wayside exhibits, trail markers.

Advantages:

- Weatherproof and never fades
- Durable and scratch resistant
- Sharp, crisp text and line art
- Reproduces black-and-white photos
- Does not require framing or backing

Disadvantages:

- Moderate cost: $250-$400 per sq. ft.
- Limited to anodized colors, like bronze, gold, silver, black, red, green, and blue

Arapaho National Wildlife Refuge, Colorado

Photo courtesy of Interpretive Graphics: *www.interpretivegraphics.com*

Cast and Silk-Screened Metal

Metal signs are virtually indestructible. The signs often have an industrial look, making them effective for road signs, historical plaques, and memorials.

Advantages:

- Cast metal:
  - Durable, weatherproof, and vandal resistant
  - Does not require framing or backing
- Silk-screened metal:
  - Low cost: $50-$125 per sq. ft.
  - Multiple colors and photo capable

Disadvantages:

- Cast metal:
  - High cost: $500-$1000 per sq. ft.
  - Limited to large letters, simple line drawings, and few colors. No photos
- Silk-screened metal:
  - Limited resolution
  - Commercial sign appearance

Urquhart Castle, Scotland

Cast metal panel

Routed/Carved and Sandblasted Wood

Zoo Frankfurt, Frankfurt, Germany

"Wood signs blend in with natural environments, trees, foliage, shrubbery, stone, or water. Beautiful landscapes and architecture are least disturbed by unobtrusive, wood signs. As wood signs age, they impart an impression of permanence."

Patrick Spielman
Making Wood Signs

Since the very first parks opened, wooden signs have been used to provide visitors with information and inspiration. Routed/carved or sandblasted wood conveys a sense of natural beauty, fitting into most landscapes. The rustic and informal qualities of wood are inviting and tell visitors that this site is an outdoor, recreational experience.

Best Uses:
Where rustic, natural appearance is important.

Options:
Routed/carved and sandblasted.

Wood is commonly used for entrance signs, trailheads, and wayfinding. Due to its limited graphic capabilities, however, wood is usually not the best choice for interpretive panels or wayside exhibits.

Advantages:
• Natural—blend with landscape
• Three-dimensional, can be shaped and carved
• Each sign is different
• Age gracefully
• Convey endurance and permanence as they weather
• Absorb gunshot
• More easily constructed and repaired in-house

Denali National Park and Preserve, Alaska

Disadvantages:
• Moderate cost. Routed/carved signs cost $125+ per sq. ft. Sandblasted signs cost $160+ per sq. ft. Price depends on detail of carving/painting.
• More construction effort than other signs
• Copies require equal effort
• Easily carved by vandals
• Detailed graphics difficult and less durable

The bear was cut, carved, and glued to the sign face.

Alaskan signs must absorb gunshot. Wood is the natural choice.

Fabrication Process—Routed/Carved Wood:

Professional wooden signs can be fabricated in-house, saving production costs. Even if purchased from a company initially, the signs can be maintained in-house with a bit of sandpaper, paint, and finish.

Creativity, patience, and a few simple tools can result in professional-appearing signs. The only limitation to your creativity is the need for uniformity in your sign system. Sign supports, panels, and faces should be similar in color, typeface, and material.

1. Tools and Materials

At a minimum, you will need a router, sharp bits, and clamps. Materials may be as basic as wood, exterior glue, and paint.

2. Gluing and Clamping

Schmeeckle Reserve cedar sign shop, Wisconsin

Panels should be clamped and glued with an exterior glue. The larger the surface area of the sign, the thicker the wood. On large panels, threaded rods inserted through the wood assure durability.

3. Image Transfer

Every routed sign begins with a pattern, text, and graphics that are transferred to a wooden sign face. Text and images can be generated with printers. Images can be copies of photographs or original art.

Transfer the pattern with an overhead projector to produce the desired size. Or print out the pattern at

full-size with a large-format printer and trace it on the sign face with carbon paper.

Some sign makers use templates and stencils for lettering. However, these devices often produce a sterile, institutional look.

4. Routing

When routing signs, choose a sharp, appropriate bit and maintain control with a shallow cut pulling the router toward you. A good light source is essential to accurately follow lines. Ear and eye protection are a must.

Schmeeckle Reserve cedar sign shop, Wisconsin

5. Carving

A hand-carved effect is achieved by routing around a drawing and then chiseling the edges.

"Dremel tools" and other rotary cutters speed up sculpting and allow inexperienced carvers to do detailed work.

6. Finishing

High quality sign paints pay for themselves in lower maintenance. Water sealers and other finishes protect sign faces, but may not be desirable for rustic signs.

This sign was created by a university student in her first attempt.

Fabrication Process— Sandblasted Wood:

Sandblasted signs accentuate wood grain and create a three-dimensional effect. It is a simple process of blasting sand on the panel through a high pressure air system. A commercial masking material is cut to create a stencil and prevents abrasion of the wood under it. Sandblasted signs can be even easier to make than routed/carved signs.

Callaway Gardens, Georgia

Glenmore Forest Park, Scotland

Photos courtesy of 3M Corporation

1. A stencil is cut in Scotch Brand Letter Perfect material.

2. The resilient rubber backing shields the desired relief areas as they are sandblasted.

3. The stencil produces a clean and sharp-edged relief.

Back-Screened Clear Plastics

Text and images are silk-screened in reverse onto the back of clear durable plastics such as Lexan or Tuffak. The plastic is mounted onto a variety of backgrounds, including aluminum, fiberglass, and wood composites.

Advantages:
- Clear plastic can be purchased from many different companies
- Text and images are protected under the plastic
- Will last for 8-10 years
- Moderate cost: $150-$200 per sq. ft.

Disadvantages:
- Plastic scratches easily
- May have a temporary appearance
- Price increases as number of colors increase
- Graphics limited to line art and half-tone photos

Municipal Dock, Escanaba, Michigan

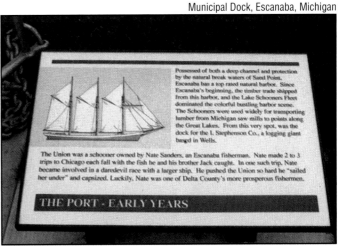

Photo courtesy of Genesis Graphics: *www.genesisgraphicsinc.com*

This sign is made of back-screened Lexan and backed with enameled aluminum.

Silk-Screened Wood Composites

Medium Density Overlay (MDO) or High Density Overlay (HDO) plywood is an inexpensive alternative for wayside exhibits and signs. Text and graphics are silk-screened over painted enamel.

Advantages:
- MDO and HDO plywood available through any lumber company
- Can be constructed by local sign shops
- Can produce duplicates for reduced price
- Low to moderate cost: $80-$130 per sq. ft.

Disadvantages:
- Less vandal resistant than other panel materials
- Temporary appearance
- Price increases as number of colors increase
- Graphics limited to line art and half-tone black-and-white photos

Granite Mountain, Montana

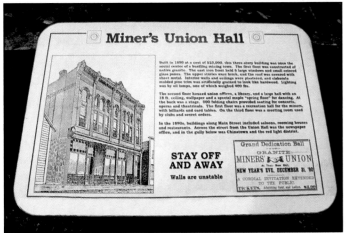

Stone

Words and text can be etched or carved into marble, limestone, granite, or other types of stone. Stone signs blend well with historic or geologically significant sites, while providing superior durability.

Anza Borrego State Park, California

Courtesy of Stone Imagery: *www.stoneimagery.com*

San Diego Zoo, California

Courtesy of Stone Imagery:
www.stoneimagery.com

Best Uses:
Memorials, battlefields, cemeteries, geologic sites

Advantages:
- Very durable and vandal resistant. Will last 15-20 years
- Words and line art are carved into the surface, so they cannot fade
- Stone naturally attracts tactile interaction
- Native stone can be used to enhance theme

Disadvantages:
- Moderate cost: $200-$350 per sq. ft.
- Limited to natural stone color, but engravings can be colored with durable Lithochrome stains
- Graphics limited to line art and half-toned black-and-white photographs
- Costs of duplicates usually remains high
- Moderately difficult to mount

Cast fiberglass has the appearance of carved wood, but requires less maintenance.

Colorado

Ceramic cast relief figures add texture to this sign.

California

Miami Metro Zoo, Florida

Cast concrete is durable and blends well with some sites.

Cast Materials

Cast concrete, ceramics, fiberglass, and plastics are durable materials for signs that have three-dimensional qualities.

Advantages:
- Durable and require less maintenance than other types of materials
- Can be molded into tactile elements on wayside exhibits
- Can be made to look like wood, stone, or other more expensive native materials
- Price depends on type of material and detail of casting

Disadvantages:
- Must be carefully selected to fit into the site. Could have a "fake" appearance
- Usually moderate to high cost

Laminated Prints

San Antonia Missions National Historic Park, Texas

Laminated printing is a quick and inexpensive method of producing interpretive signage. Signs are printed onto paper with special UV-resistant inks. The print is sealed between sheets of UV-resistant laminate. It is then mounted to a variety of backgrounds, including aluminum, plastic, and wood.

Advantages:
- Can be fabricated in-house or by a local sign company
- Very inexpensive: $10-$30 per sq. ft. or less
- Quick turn-around time of a few days
- Works well for temporary or seasonal exhibits
- Can be used to test the effectiveness of a sign before fabricating with more expensive materials
- Produces sharp text and high-resolution, full-color graphics

Disadvantages:
- Not suggested for permanent signage; it has a temporary appearance
- Can last up to 3 years outdoors with UV-inks and laminate, but usually much less
- Very susceptible to vandalism if not protected beneath clear plastic or held in a frame
- Glare is often a problem

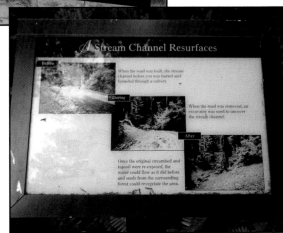
Redwoods National Park, California

Panel Tips

- Avoid inexpensive materials in large rectangles, such as a 4'x8' sheet of plywood. This creates a billboard appearance.

- Avoid square panels. A 5:3 or 5:4 ratio is more visually appealing.

- Use panel materials that are appropriate to your site. Avoid highly reflective materials that create glare. Choose materials that are vandal, insect, wildlife, salt, and water resistant.

- Select panel materials based on:
  - Long term maintenance requirements/vandalism risk.
  - Budget limitations or cost/benefit.
  - Color and graphic needs.

Avoid standard rectangle sizes.

Summary of Panel Materials

	High Pressure Laminate	Fiberglass Embedment: Digital	Fiberglass Embedment: Screened	Porcelain Enamel	Color-Embed Anodized Aluminum	Photo Etched Anodized Aluminum
Graphics and Color						
Graphics Capability/ Resolution	Very good	Very good	Very good	Excellent	Very good	Good, line art, half-tones
Color Capability	4-color digital	4-color digital	4-color screen	4-color screen	4-color screen	Anodized colors
Image/Color Retention Over Time	Good	Good	Good	Excellent	Excellent	Excellent
Photo Reproduction Capability	Very good, full color	Good, full color	Very good, full color	Excellent, full color	Very good, full color	Good, half-tone, black-and-white
Material Durability						
Life Expectancy in Serviceable Condition	Good, 10-20 years	Good, 5-10 years	Good, 8-10 years	Excellent, 40+ years	Excellent, 40+ years	Excellent, 40+ years
Scratch/Abrasion Resistance	Very good	Very good	Very good	Excellent	Very good	Very good
Cracking/ Peeling/Warping Resistance	Good	Good	Good	Excellent	Excellent	Excellent
Maintenance Needed	Bi-annual wash/wax	Bi-annual wash/wax	Bi-annual wash/wax	Annual wash/ wax	Annual wash	Annual wash
Framing Needed	≧ 1/2" No	Yes	Yes	Yes	Yes	No
Impact Resistance (Hard Blows)	Very good	Very good	Very good	Poor	Good	Fair
Graffiti Removal	Very good	Very good	Very good	Excellent	Excellent	Good
Replaceability/ Duplication	Very good, inexpensive	Excellent, duplicates	Excellent, duplicates	Poor	Good	Poor
Typical Applications						
Wayside Exhibits/ Trail Panels	Very good	Very good	Very good	Excellent	Very good	Good
Site and Facility Identification	Good	Good	Good	Good	Very good	Very good
Memorials/Plaques	Poor	Poor	Poor	Poor	Good	Excellent
Identification Labels	Good	Good	Good	Good	Excellent	Very good
Cost Range per sq. ft. (2006 prices)	Low: $50-$70	Low: $40-$60	High: $250-$530	High: $300-$600	Mod: $100-$150	High: $250-$400

Revised chart based on A Guide to Materials for Interpretive Sign Fabrication *by Richard F. Ostergaard, USDA-Forest Service, Denver, Colorado*

Metal: Cast	Metal: Screened	Wood: Routed/Carved	Wood: Sandblasted	Back-Screened Plastic	Wood Composite: Screened	Stone Etching	Laminated Prints
Poor	Poor	Carved, routed, painted	Excellent letters and line art	Good	Good	Good	Very good
Painted	4-color screen	Painted, stained	Painted, stained	4-color screen	4-color screen	Lithochrome paints	4-color digital
Excellent	Good	Fair	Fair	Good	Fair	Excellent	Poor
N/A	Fair, half-tone	N/A	N/A	Good, full color	Fair, half-tone, black-and-white	Fair, half-tone, black-and-white	Very good, full color
Excellent, 40+ years	Good, 10-15 years	Fair, 5-6 years, can refurbish	Fair, 5-6 years, can refurbish	Good, 8-10 years	Fair, 4-6 years	Very good, 15-20 years	Poor, 1-3 years with UV protect
Excellent	Poor	Good	Good	Good	Fair	Excellent	Poor
Excellent	Very good	Excellent	Excellent	≥ 1/2" Good	Good	Excellent	Fair
None	Bi-annual wash	Stain every 5-6 years	Stain every 5-6 years	Bi-annual wash	Bi-annual wash	None	Bi-annual wash
No	≥ 1/2" No	No	No	Yes	No	No	Yes
Fair	Fair	Good	Good	Good	Poor	Poor	Poor
Poor	Good	Fair	Fair	Very good	Good	Poor	Good
Poor	Fair	Poor	Poor	Poor	Fair	Poor	Very good, inexpensive
Poor	Poor	Poor	Poor	Good	Good	Good	Good
Fair	Poor	Excellent	Excellent	Fair	Very good	Good	Poor
Excellent	Poor	Poor	Fair	Poor	Poor	Very Good	Poor
Good	Fair	Good	Very Good	Good	Good	Very Good	Fair
Very High: $500-$1000	Low-Mod: $50-$125	Mod-High: $125+	Mod-High: $160+	Mod: $150-$200	Low-Mod: $80-$130	High: $200-$350	Very Low: $10-$30

Sign Supports

Supports do more than hold up the sign. They can also imply permanence and respect for a site and provide a link with site features.

Supports are aesthetically pleasing when they relate to their purpose and surroundings. Real charm is a result of creativeness, imagination, and sensitivity to the site.

The physical quality of supports should have a harmonious relationship with the natural environment, buildings, or the site theme.

Tatra Mountain National Park, Poland

This trail closed sign in Tatra Mountain National Park, Poland, uses carefully chosen natural timbers.

Hawaii Volcanoes National Park, Hawaii

Native materials are often used to mirror the site features.

Hans Suter Wildlife Area, Texas

Supports may be more visual than physical. These heavy timbers were needed to visually balance the thick sign face.

Redwood National and State Parks, California

Colors and materials can be selected to complement the site.

Zion National Park, Utah

Padre Island National Seashore, Texas

Color and landforms are reflected in this entrance sign.

The sand dunes of Padre Island are suggested in this support.

Corkscrew Swamp Audubon Sanctuary, Florida

Cape Pepetua Scenic Area, Oregon

Natural supports and plantings are a way to frame signs in nature preserves.

Vertical timbers repeat the tree patterns. Their boldness emphasizes this wayside's significance.

Aransas National Wildlife Refuge, Texas

Nez Perce National Historic Park, Idaho

Mammoth Cave National Park, Kentucky

Symbolic supports can reinforce the themes of a site.

Standard Bases for Wayside Exhibits

Standardized frames and mounts, based on National Park Service designs, are affordable solutions for holding panels.

Devil's Lake State Park, Wisconsin

Upright mount. Vertical panels command more attention than angled mounts.

Diamond Head State Monument, Hawaii

Wall mount frame. Attaches to the side of a building or kiosk.

Arches National Park, Utah

Low profile cantilevered base. The edge of the frame extends to the front of the legs.

Sanibel-Captiva Conservation Foundation, Florida

Single pedestal mount. Plate attaches directly to a self-supporting panel (no frame).

Rogue-Umpqua National Scenic Byway, Oregon

Low profile traditional base. The edge of the frame extends beyond the legs.

Tomorrow River State Trail, Wisconsin

An aluminum frame attached to 4"x4" wood posts is an inexpensive mounting alternative.

Crater Lake National Park, Oregon

Low profile frame. Mounts to a rock wall or boardwalk railing.

Thematic Mounting Options

A stylized base that relates to the panel's theme can reinforce the interpretive message.

Taylor Creek Visitor Center, Nevada

Beinn Eighe National Nature Reserve, Scotland

Oregon Islands National Wildlife Refuge, Oregon

Wayside Exhibit Support Recommendations

- The panel must be accessible to all readers.
  - For angled frames, install at a height of 30-34" from the bottom of the exhibit panel to the finished grade.
  - Use frames that hold panels at an angle of 30° or 45°. The steeper 45° angle works best for viewing from a car.
  - For vertical exhibits, install at a height of 24-28" from the bottom of the panel.

- Sign bases can be buried in the ground or mounted directly to concrete or boardwalks.

- Poured concrete or cross-members buried in the ground discourage vandalism.

- Choose materials that are resistant to the elements and protect the panel from vandalism. Powder-coated aluminum is commonly used for frames. Legs are often made of powder-coated aluminum, steel, or wood.

- Select a framing option that is unobtrusive to the site, blends with the landscape, and is thematic with the interpretation.

Kiosks

A roof over a bulletin board or wayside exhibit draws the visitor into the shelter of the overhang. It creates a defined space where people feel protected.

A kiosk can serve as a staging area to a site, concentrating orientation, rules, safety advice, and interpretive messages into one structure.

Nachusa Grasslands, Illinois

Petroglyph National Monument, New Mexico

Inexpensive kiosks can be constructed with 4"x4" posts. However, the structure often looks temporary and may not blend with the landscape.

Kiosks constructed with larger sized timbers appear more durable and permanent.

Logan Canyon National Scenic Byway, Utah

This well-designed kiosk on the Logan Canyon National Scenic Byway attracts attention, sets a tone for the interpretation, and replicates indigenous materials.

Other kiosks along the byway use the same design elements, increasing recognition for drivers.

Moody Air Force Base, Georgia

Padre Island National Seashore, Texas

A roof over a trailhead and orientation sign is an invitation to stop before starting on the trail.

A complex series of signs and wayside exhibits can be organized and clustered in a kiosk.

Green Circle Trail, Stevens Point, Wisconsin

Beinn Eighe National Nature Reserve, Scotland

This urban trail kiosk was built large to stand out from surrounding buildings.

The use of native materials, such as rocks, logs, and sod roofs, warmly invites visitors to experience the signage within.

Sign Problems

Regardless of the panels and bases you choose, vandalism, harsh natural elements, and poor installation can negatively impact your signs.

Regular maintenance keeps signs at their best. Some minor vandalism and weathering can be repaired for little or no cost.

If a sign panel cannot be repaired, it should be removed. Poor looking signs will detract from a visitor's experience.

Vandalism

Permanent markers, spray paint, lipstick, and crayons can be removed from most quality materials with organic solvents or mineral spirits.

Minor scratches can usually be buffed out of materials with polymer-based car wax.

Fading

All materials will fade over time. Panels that have more direct contact with sunlight (no shade, facing south in the Northern Hemisphere, high elevations) or are consistently blasted with sand (beaches, des-

erts) will fade much faster. If fading is an issue, consider using more durable materials such as porcelain enamel, stone, or metal, or moving the sign to a protected location.

Wildlife

Badlands National Park, South Dakota

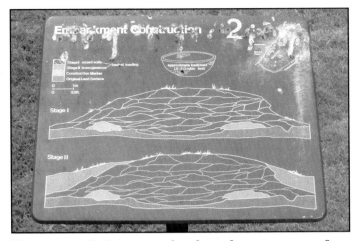

Signs installed in grassland or desert areas often attract perching birds. Evidence left behind can obscure the interpretive message. Porcupines and squirrels may chew on wooden signs.

Stringing a thin wire at the highest point of a sign discourages birds from perching on them. Many wildlife problems can be avoided by modifying the frame or choosing different materials.

Message Access

Avoid using materials that glare and reflect.

Install panels at a height that provides easy viewing for all visitors.

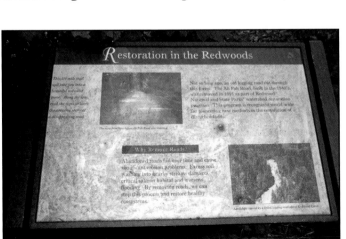

Regularly clean panels to prolong their life.

Plan panel sizes that do not block views of the site.

Ice Age National Scenic Trail, Wisconsin

Chapter 6:
Planning Wayside Exhibits

Interpretive Plans

Since wayside exhibits are only one method of connecting the interests of visitors to the meanings of the resource, it is essential that they are derived from a holistic planning process. Interpretive plans provide a vision for the future of interpretation and visitor experiences at your site.

Interpretive plans address both non-personal services (media and facilities) and personal services (programs and personal contacts). Plans match interpretive media to themes and messages to ensure that they are the best choices for making resource-visitor connections.

Planning is the process of developing effective wayside exhibits based on:
1. The mission and goals of the organization or agency.
2. The interests and needs of the visitors.
3. The unique and meaningful features of the resource.

The Planning Triangle

Answering the three basic questions of "Why? Who? What?" sets the foundation for developing effective interpretive media.

Why? Analyze the mission and goals of your organization or agency. Some mission statements are in writing, but also look at the unstated goals.

Who? Understand and listen to the visitor. Use surveys, focus groups, or informal interviews. Why do people come to this place? What do they want to know? Learn

about their questions, feelings, impressions. Take the perspective of as many of your visitors as possible. How does this place look from the perspective of a child or a person in a wheelchair?

What? Develop an intimate understanding of the site and resources. Immerse yourself in the site. Are there events, landscapes, or objects that can link people to meaningful feelings, ideas, or insights? What stories are told about this place? Read. Talk to people who know.

Why? Mission

Interpretive Plan

Media and Methods

Who? Visitor

What? Resource

Writing Themes and Messages

Themes are a synthesis of "Why? Who? and What?" They are the "big ideas" that organize the stories we will tell through our wayside exhibits. They create a framework for message and media choices, and help place resources and events into a meaningful context for visitors.

A compelling interpretive theme:
• Is a single concise sentence.
• Links tangible resources to intangible meanings.
• Directs the messages that are to be included on signage.

A **primary theme** is the main idea for all of the media and programs that will be developed for a site, trail, or byway.

Sub-themes split the primary theme into several broad categories, making the ideas more workable.

Messages are the specific stories that can be told. They directly relate to each sub-theme.

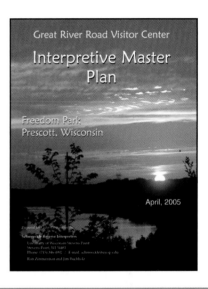

Example: Great River Road Visitor Center at Prescott, WI
Interpretive Master Plan developed by Schmeeckle Reserve Interpreters

Primary theme

Prescott, a classic River Town and gateway to the Great River Road, is a gathering place where rivers, wildlife, and people blend into a dynamic living community rich in history and grand scenery.

Sample Sub-themes and Messages

Sub-theme 1: The Mississippi and St. Croix Rivers are ribbons of life for people, plants, and animals.

Messages (samples):
1. The narrowing of the Mississippi valley at Prescott funnels thousands of diverse migrating birds every spring and fall.
2. The Mississippi Flyway is a migration corridor for 40% of North America's waterfowl and shorebirds.

Sub-theme 3: The Mississippi and St. Croix are working rivers that have sustained people's livelihoods throughout history.

Messages (samples):
1. By 1898, there were nearly 50 button factories on the Upper Mississippi.
2. Freshwater pearls were commonly found in the Upper Mississippi, and even served as legal tender for drinks in the bars of Winona, Minnesota.

Sub-theme 2: The history of the Mississippi and St. Croix River transportation is a dramatic story reflecting the rivers' economic and commercial importance.

Messages (samples):
1. Seven steamboats stopped at the Prescott levee every day in 1855.
2. Cut logs were lashed into massive floating rafts, 1,600 feet long by 300 feet wide.

Sub-theme 4: Mississippi River towns, like Prescott, reflect mid-19th century life.

Messages (samples):
1. River towns, like Prescott, had street grids that were oriented to the Mississippi rather than north/south or east/west.
2. In 1851, Philander Prescott obtained title to about 200 acres of land at his original claim.

Developing a Conceptual Media Plan

Throughout the initial stages of planning, consider different media and program choices that would best connect visitors to the meaningful stories of your site.

Sometimes, wayside exhibits are not the best option. Few visitors to secluded wilderness areas, for example, would welcome the intrusion of an interpretive panel.

If signs are chosen to help communicate the interpretive messages, it is important to decide:

- The purpose of each sign.
- How the sign will create intellectual and emotional connections.
- How the sign relates to the themes and messages of the site.
- Where the sign will be placed.

- What graphic design standards will be used to unify the signs.

A Conceptual Media Plan directly addresses these ideas, showing connections to the holistic planning process.

For every conceptual sign, you should include:

Purpose: Why is the sign important to telling the story of the site?

Objectives: How effective will the sign be at providing the intended interpretive experience?
- **Intellectual:** What will visitors learn? This includes factual information that can be tested.
- **Emotional:** What will visitors feel or experience?
- **Behavioral:** What will visitors do while reading the sign (read, view, touch, smell)? What will visitors be motivated to do *after* experiencing the sign?

Themes and Messages: Which themes and messages does this sign directly interpret? Using a coding system ("2.4" = "Sub-theme 2, Message 4") can simplify this listing.

Location: Where will this sign be installed so it is visible, accessible, and connects to an object, landscape, or event?

Description and Conceptual Rendering: A detailed description and sketch or rendering help readers to visualize the finished sign.

Draft panel, Great River Road Visitor Center, Prescott, Wisconsin

Example: Migration Corridor

Purpose: To tell the dramatic story of migration along the Mississippi River, connecting visitors to unique bird species that can be seen from the site.

Objectives (samples):
- **Intellectual:** Visitors will learn that the Mississippi River valley narrows at Prescott, funneling thousands of migrating birds.
- **Emotional:** Visitors will be excited by the possibility of seeing uncommon birds like tundra swans, white pelicans, and loons.
- **Behavioral:** Visitors will search the skies for migrating birds and visit another site on the scenic byway to observe tundra swans.

Themes and Messages: 1.1, 1.3, 1.4, 1.9, 2.3, 4.7

Location: Main Viewing Deck, connected to the visitor center.

Graphic Design Standards

Develop graphic design standards to unify signage throughout the site. These standards ensure that current and future signs will fit into the design scheme. Standards should include:
- Shape and size
- Color: Choose a universal color scheme that fabricators will recognize (like PANTONE).

- Typography: Font types, styles, and sizes for each text component.
- Unifying elements: Logos, title bars, side bars, tint boxes, and other visual elements that will be replicated on every sign.
- Panel material(s): Materials that are appropriate for signs based on cost, durability, and aesthetics.

Example: Wayside Exhibit Design Standards, Great River Road Visitor Center

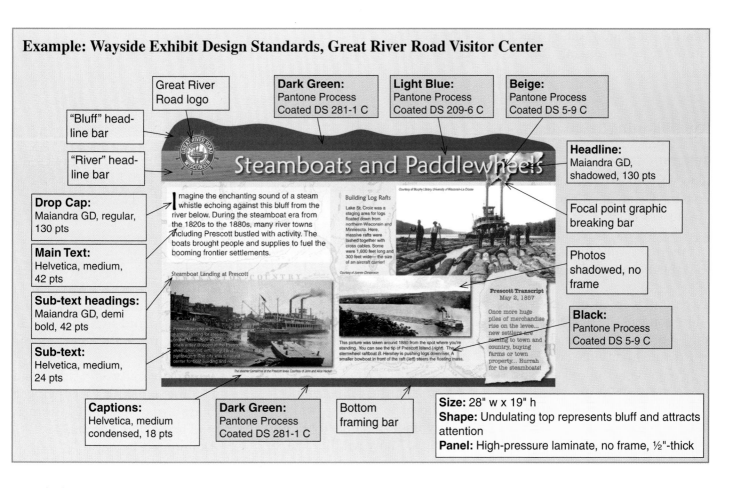

Writing, Design, Fabrication, and Installation

Based on the Planning Triangle, Themes and Messages, and Conceptual Media Plan, wayside exhibits can be written and designed that connect visitors to the meaningful stories of your site.

Modern computers and software allow interpreters to design signage in-house, saving on the cost of a professional designer. However, many organizations and agencies will choose to hire an outside designer who can make more efficient use of time and provide a higher level of expertise. Regardless, interpreters or managers should be involved at all stages of the process to ensure that the integrity of the interpretive messages are maintained.

For more information about designing signs and writing messages, see Chapters 3 and 4.

For more information about fabrication and installation, see Chapter 5.

Case Studies in Wayside Planning

Black River Marsh Boardwalk

Even a small signage project requires a solid foundation of planning. Schmeeckle Reserve Interpreters was asked to design wayside exhibits for a short boardwalk loop in Kohler-Andrae State Park, Wisconsin.

Kohler-Andrae State Park, Wisconsin

The Planning Triangle

Why?

The written mission of the Wisconsin Department of Natural Resources is:

To preserve, protect, effectively manage, and maintain Wisconsin's natural resources.

Park staff were interviewed to explore some of the unwritten goals of the project. These included:

- Provide additional recreational experiences for visitors.
- Create a walkway that the park naturalist can utilize for teaching wetland programs.
- Develop a connection between park visitors and the marsh.

Who?

Interviews with park staff, general observations, and demographic data revealed the primary audiences.

- **Campers:** Primarily family groups in the campground adjacent to the boardwalk.
- **Day users:** Primarily family groups. Many wildlife watchers.

What?

Immersing ourselves in the site with canoes and hip waders provided an intimate view of the marsh.

- Great diversity of wildlife, including muskrats, red-winged blackbirds, sandhill cranes, and great blue herons.
- Dominated by cattails, sedges, and purple loosestrife.

Themes and Messages

Based on our initial study, we decided to avoid the common "Benefits of a Wetland" theme. Most visitors here have a stronger interest in discovering the wildlife unique to this marsh.

The **primary theme** was crafted based on the "Why? Who? What?"

Four **sub-themes** were developed from the primary theme. Since the scope of the project was so focused, each sub-theme represented one interpretive panel. **Messages** were written for each sub-theme.

Conceptual Media Plan

A **purpose**, specific **objectives**, and **location** were developed for each sign.

The design standards were chosen to encourage a sense of discovery and social interaction. Large cut-out animals in dynamic poses attract attention. Short messages next to each picture present fun facts, and a magnifying glass encourages younger visitors to "look closer." The simple typeface makes the sign open and readable.

Writing, Design, and Fabrication

The panels were fabricated with 1/8"-thick high pressure laminate. They were installed in aluminum cantilevered frames bolted to the boardwalk deck. The entrance sign was constructed with cedar, providing a natural look for the interpretive trail.

Primary theme: The Black River Marsh, a cattail-dominated riverine wetland, offers an exciting opportunity to view unique plants and animals that are adapted to life in the water.

Sub-theme 1: Like trees in a forest, dense stands of cattails provide shelter, protection, and food for many wildlife species.

Messages (samples):
1. Male red-winged blackbirds arrive in early spring to find the best nesting sites.
2. Marsh wrens hunt insects near the base of cattails.
3. European beetles and weevils were released in the Black River Marsh to control the spread of purple loosestrife, an exotic flower.

Conceptual Media Plan: "In the Cattails" Panel

Purpose: To illustrate the importance of cattails to the marsh ecosystem, and introduce the negative impacts of purple loosestrife.

Objectives (samples):
- **Intellectual:** Visitors will learn that many animals, including red-winged blackbirds, marsh wrens, and muskrats, depend on cattails for survival.
- **Emotional:** Visitors will feel amazed by the many ways cattails are used by wetland wildlife.
- **Behavioral:** Visitors will look for muskrat houses, red-winged blackbird nests, and European loosestrife beetles. Visitors will listen for the calls of red-winged blackbirds and marsh wrens.

Themes and Messages: All messages under Sub-theme 1.

Location: Southern loop of boardwalk with view over vast area of cattails and muskrat houses.

Kohler-Andrae State Park, Wisconsin

Sub-theme 2: The Black River is a slowly moving channel of water deeper than the surrounding marshland, providing habitat for waterfowl and fish.

Messages (samples):
1. Only hardy fish, like carp and bullheads can survive in the low oxygen conditions.
2. Sandhill cranes return each spring to nest in the marsh.

Conceptual Media Plan: "The Black River"

Purpose: To show the connection between the Black River and its marsh, and how some wildlife species depend on the deeper channel to survive.

Objectives (samples):
• **Intellectual:** Visitors will learn how the Black River got its name, where it flows, and about common animals both above and below the surface.

• **Emotional:** Visitors will feel that they are part of a much larger community connected by the river.
• **Behavioral:** Visitors will look for waterfowl, wading birds, and fish in the river, and listen for the trumpeting of sandhill cranes.

Themes and Messages: All messages under Sub-theme 2.

Location: Northern Black River overlook.

Sub-theme 3: Life below the marsh's water surface enriches and supports the entire marsh ecosystem.

Messages (samples):
1. The rich, organic muck of a marsh supports a great diversity of plants and animals.
2. Dragonfly nymphs are fierce predators with specialized lower lips used to capture prey.

Conceptual Media Plan: "Below the Surface"

Purpose: To immerse visitors in the rarely experienced underwater world of the marsh, and introduce them to some of the unique animals that support the wetland ecosystem.

Objectives (samples):
• **Intellectual:** Visitors will learn that life flourishes under the water of a marsh, which supports larger animals above the surface.

• **Emotional:** Visitors will be intrigued by the flurry of activity occurring below their feet.
• **Behavioral:** Visitors will smell the methane gas of a marsh and look for insects on the surface of the water.

Themes and Messages: All messages under Sub-theme 3.

Location: Southern Black River overlook, where visitors can observe life beneath the water.

Mount Saint Helens National Volcanic Monument

Mount St. Helens National Volcanic Monument, Washington

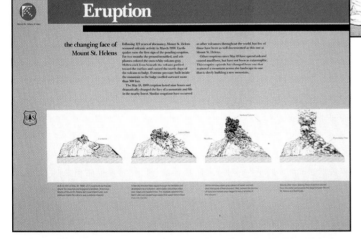

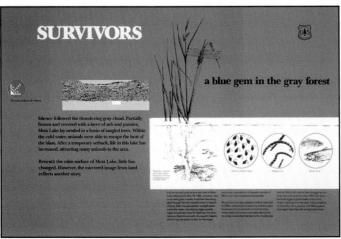

The eruption of Mount Saint Helens on May 18, 1980 provided an unparalleled opportunity to answer the questions of a public hungry for information. The story of catastrophic geologic forces, human tragedy, and the tenacity of life are the elements of a compelling story.

The interpretive staff at the newly created Mount Saint Helens National Volcanic Monument had to act quickly to provide accurate, yet concise information to visitors on the site. Wayside exhibits were an important part of a comprehensive interpretive plan.

A team was formed which included a supervisory interpreter, writers, artists, graphic designers, landscape architects, and representatives from the supervisor's office.

The writing team took a holistic approach. It is a model that you may wish to follow. You will be rewarded with signs that answer important visitor questions in a consistent and thematic way.

Steps in Planning the Mount Saint Helens Interpretation

Develop a Common Vision

Take the team to the sites to be interpreted. Try to look at the site as though you are a first-time visitor. This visit can give you insight into the questions and feelings that visitors might have. Everyone's thoughts and emotions should be recorded. Gain insight by observing visitors and interviewing them.

Brainstorm

While the impressions are fresh and still developing, brainstorm the possibilities as a team. It is important to maintain a free-wheeling, non-judgmental atmosphere. Even the wildest ideas should be recorded. Identify a brainstorming facilitator who records ideas on an easel for all to see.

The core purposes for each sign is explored. "The visitor should feel frailty of life and our own lack of power and control." "The visitor should know the scale of destruction in those first few moments of the blast."

Research and Inventory

Research is necessary to develop your stories and insure accuracy. The team should collect reports and photographs that document the facts. Identify and interview people who have special knowledge about the site. These may be experts or locals. Record these interviews in a notebook. Listen carefully for metaphors, analogies, and phrases that your resource specialists use. These may give a breath of life to otherwise cold abstractions.

Set Final Themes and Objectives

This step verifies that the team is focusing on the same big ideas. Identify specific themes that will be developed in your interpretive signs. Write objectives for each sign. Objectives should reflect the emotions and knowledge you wish to convey or the actions you wish your visitors to take. Themes and objectives consider the visitor, the stories of the site, the agency, and effective methods of communication.

Craft the Message

Your message is a wedding of words and visuals. Each affects and amplifies the other. Graphic artists and writers must work together.

The Mount Saint Helens team wrote a series of drafts, each a refinement of the preceding, until the team agreed that both art and text told the story in a concise and stimulating way.

Construct a Mock-up

Construct an inexpensive mock-up for visitors to test. From cosmetics to airplanes, products are tested before they go into production. A field test of your sign can tell you if you are connecting with the visitor.

Observe visitors as they interact with your sign. Do they read they entire message? Talk to them. Do they still have questions that aren't being answered? Have they been moved or provoked? Do they have any suggestions?

Use their suggestions to adjust your message. Once a sign is set in fiberglass, metal, or wood, changes are unlikely.

San Diego Wild Animal Park

Zoos also rely on interpretive signs to communicate with visitors. It is rare, if not impossible, to interpret the dynamic behavior of animals with signs in the wild. In controlled settings, signs placed at observation points can answer common and predictable questions.

San Diego Wild Animal Park consistently achieves high quality in their interpretive signs. They have created a graphics manual so that all staff members work from a common philosophy. Parts of this manual are reproduced on page 107.

San Diego Wild Animal Park, California

Visitor involvement is a primary goal for San Diego Wild Animal Park.

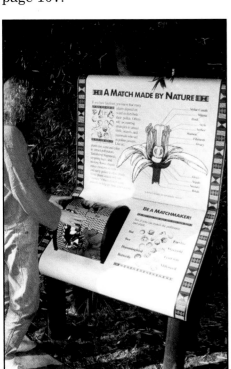

"A Match Made by Nature" challenges the visitor to spin the wheels and match pollinators with their flower.

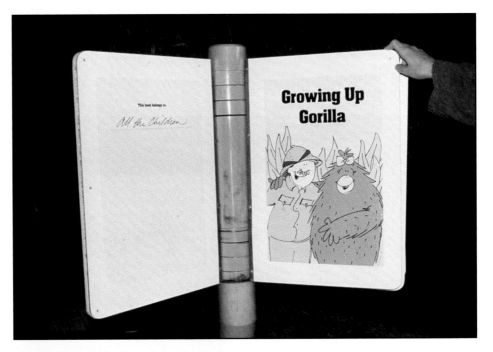

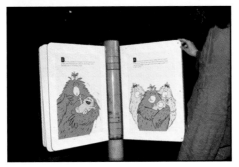

Wild Animal Park signs engage children and adults. The storybook format of "Growing up Gorilla" is particularly appropriate for younger children.

The Wild Animal Park is renowned for its breeding program of endangered species. Several panels tell that story.

Engaging titles, brief messages, and dramatic graphics ensure a high Fraction of Selection for Wild Animal Park panels.

Signs are placed at strategic viewing points.

Longer messages are placed along the tramway waiting line.

Excerpts from Wild Animal Park Manual

This graphics manual has helped the San Diego Wild Animal Park achieve uniformity in content and graphics. Quality is achieved by employing professional writers and artists. Contracted writers and artists use the manual to learn the park philosophy, sign parameters, and production standards.

Educational signs are silent yet eloquent hosts to guests...

The graphics content will convey information in ways that... inspire our guests...

The Wild Animal Park is perhaps the only zoo that was created for animals, not for people...

These are characteristics of visitors to the San Diego Wild Animal Park...

The fictitious person behind our graphics voice: Is succinct... Is visionary about wildlife...

**Content Guidelines
for
Graphics**

Education Department
San Diego Wild Animal Park

Table of Contents

Steps to Include in Content Development

1. **Identify visitors' questions/comments about the topic.**
   - listen/eavesdrop at the exhibit
   - ask visitors what they would like to know
   - put a tape recorder or comment board at the exhibit
   - ask keepers and other employees what visitors inquire about
   - ask tour guides what visitors ask them
   - brainstorm questions with the exhibit team

2. **Use questions and directions to psychologically project visitors into the exhibit.**
   - e.g., compare your hand to a gorilla's (handprint)
   - e.g., which is the female?

3. **Plan all graphics together.**
   - directional
   - interpretive
   - donor
   - plant

4. **Include different levels/types of information.**
   - illustrations
   - peep holes
   - touchables
   - details
   - stories
   - video
   - sounds
   - photographs
   - appropriate humor

5. **Select topics and develop text that is imagable.**

6. **Offer different kinds of physical experiences.**
   - look closely
   - peek
   - reach
   - push
   - lift
   - feel
   - listen
   - find
   - turn
   - wonder
   - smell
   - touch

7. **Get visitors to read to each other.**
   - use large type
   - place graphic at eye level
   - use short sentences and paragraphs
   - ask questions
   - use catchy phrases
   - use humor

8. **Make the text readable.**
   - refer to things the visitor can see
   - use words that direct the visitor to observe and/or participate
   - answer commonly-asked questions
   - offer games and humor
   - give feedback
   - organize—chronological order; cause and effect; problem, analysis, solution; order of importance; part
   - tell a story
   - correct misconceptions
   - use subheads—sentences that summarize
   - build in rhythm and internal rhyme
   - use parallelism
   - repeat
   - compare and contrast

Introduction

Educational signs are silent yet eloquent hosts to guests who visit the San Diego Wild Animal Park. When visitors approach an enclosure, enter an aviary, or wonder about a plant or animal, our graphics can stimulate ideas, answer questions, and help visitors understand our message.

Because the function of our graphics program is so important, we have developed these content guidelines. They help us create graphic content in a consistent manner, from a common point of view, and with intentional messages.

The uses of this document are primarily:
- *Training for new employees and consultants*
- *Platform for consistency for writers and editors*

Chapter 7:
Trails: Corridors to Adventure

Two roads diverged in a yellow wood,
And sorry I could not travel both
And be one traveler, long I stood
And looked down one as far as I could
To where it bent in the undergrowth.

Robert Frost
The Road Not Taken

Big Bend National Park, Texas

Designing Trails that Involve People

Trails fill fundamental needs within us. According to Charles E. Little:

> There are some who find a trailhead, or a path through the woods which curves invitingly out of sight, simply irresistible. Thoreau was such a person and before him Wordsworth. And today it's me and probably you. It is a romantic idea, surely, a reaction to the organized spaces of an industrial age, with all its square corners and square lives and intentionality. Sometimes we need just to set out, afoot or a-bike, to go where a path takes us… But when a path and a natural scene are joined, the congruence can work powerfully on our imagination. Striding across a meadow, picking one's way along a ridge, or meandering down the banks of a stream makes even ordinary landscapes somehow wonderful.

> Greenways for America

Yellowstone National Park

Big Bend National Park, Texas

Bearskin State Trail, Wisconsin

Blue Springs State Park, Florida

Mount Washburn Trail, Yellowstone National Park

When asked, people say they take trails in search of:

- Solitude
- Beauty
- New experiences
- Meaning/connectedness
- Escape from daily stresses or boredom
- Self-renewal
- A private place
- Peace
- Inspiration
- Novelty
- Comradeship
- Romance
- Challenge
- Memories

Olympic National Park, Washington

A well-designed trail offers the possibility of fulfilling these needs. But even a well-planned trail is serendipitous and subject to the whims of nature.

Sequence of season shots, Schmeeckle Reserve, Wisconsin

A trail has many moods depending on time of day, weather, or season. A trail in May, alive with migrating warblers, in June is swarming with mosquitoes. Good trail design allows for dynamic possibilities.

Ingredients for Visitor Involvement

Trail design is the process of exposing the mystery, variety, and beauty that a site has to offer. Nearly everything that engages a visitor along a trail can be classified into one or more of these three categories: mystery, variety, and beauty.

Designing for Mystery

Mystery is any feature of a trail that arouses curiosity and provokes the visitor to explore. An observer should be induced to move around the bend or over the crest of a hill to see what lies beyond. Mystery can be:

- Enticing trail names.
- Stories of artifacts or past events that occurred here.
- A trail curving around a bend out of view.
- The fragrance of a milkweed blossom.
- The lure of a cool, dark canyon.
- A vista partially screened by vegetation.
- A tantalizing view of a peak that looms in the distance.
- Light filtering through a canopy opening.
- Sunny openings in the heart of a dense forest that invite entry and exploration.
- Distant sounds of rushing water.

Lane Cove Greenway, Sydney, Australia

Overhanging sandstone frames a view of eucalyptus trees on this urban trail.

Schmeeckle Reserve, Wisconsin

Vegetation can be pruned or removed to frame vistas.

Tunnels on the Iron Mountain Road in the Black Hills are designed to frame the faces of Mount Rushmore.

A provocative trail name, direct invitation, and oyster shell shape lure the visitor onto this trail.

Big trees, a curving trail, stone steps, dramatic overlooks, and the roar of water echoing in a gorge lure walkers down this trail. The Rogue Gorge in the Rogue River National Forest is a popular wayside along the Rogue-Umpqua Scenic Byway.

Designing for Variety

Variety is any feature of a trail that provides contrast, diversity and change. We rebel against monotony. A trail through a plantation of even aged trees soon becomes boring. We enjoy the contrast of big and little trees, mixed undergrowth, forest openings, and rock outcroppings. A word of caution, however; too much variety can be chaotic and create a sense of disorder. Sometimes monotony can be induced in order to enhance or intensify a spectacular view farther along the trail.

Variety can take the form of:

- Colors of bark, leaves, flowers, and fruit.
- Textures and plant forms.
- An area exposed to wind contrasted to one that is sheltered.
- A shaded trail that opens on (or into) a sunny meadow.
- The perspective of a tower or elevated walkway.
- The smell of a sun-soaked pine forest or a prairie pothole.
- Contrasting landforms and landscape features.
- Changing habitats such as dry forest to swamps to a sandy beach.

Schmeeckle Reserve, Wisconsin

Water is mutable—it mirrors the weather and the seasons. People are captivated by its moods of ripples and waves, and its intensified reflections of storms and sunshine.

Rocky Mountain National Park, Colorado

People naturally seek the highest point possible for a view of a landscape. A panoramic view of the valley and the possibility of spotting wildlife make this vista worth a visit.

Route trails to feature the diversity of the site. Big trees inspire awe. Cathedral-like forests give a sense of shelter and are a tangible link to our primeval past. Light filtered through a canopy dances from shrubs and ferns. The forest offers a calendar of color in ephemeral flowers, bright fruit, and autumn leaves. Each layer of the forest harbors wildlife to observe.

Berard Oaks, Schmeeckle Reserve, Wisconsin

An oak savanna changes throughout the seasons. Golden prairie grasses and colorful leaves in the autumn add variety to the landscape. The open landscape stands in contrast to heavily wooded trails.

A diversity of wildlife is also attracted to the park-like setting of a savanna. Glimpsing a white-tailed deer is the highlight of many trail experiences. Wildlife encounters enrich the variety of a trail.

Designing for Beauty

Beauty may be described as grace, elegance, or harmony. Everyone recognizes beauty, but few can define it.

Most would agree that mystery and variety are attributes of beauty. There is mystery in a river meandering gracefully out of sight. There is less beauty in one that has been straightened into a channel. Variety provides excitement, but it must be balanced with our need for order. It is the tension between the stimulation of variety and the tranquility of order that gives us pleasure.

Beauty has been defined as the degree that objects and features fit with their surroundings. "Fitness" can be reflected in the dominance of natural elements (colors, forms, texture) and natural processes, and the subordination of human influences.

Human activities frequently disrupt order. An unscreened clear-cut, a dam on a fast flowing river, the constant hum of a distant highway, a power line cutting across the landscape, or a brightly colored sign lack harmony and order. A pleasing trail must screen or avoid objectionable aspects.

Braulio Carillio National Park, Costa Rica

A panoramic view offers tranquility. The convergence of land, water, and sky creates a sense of order.

Schmeeckle Reserve, Wisconsin

The harmony of nature is broken by traffic, wires, and straight lines. Vegetation can buffer objectionable sights and sounds.

Knockan Crag National Nature Reserve, Scotland

Kentucky Caverns, Kentucky

Wide open spaces with views to distant mountain peaks and valley lakes enhance the appeal of this ridge trail.

The beauty of a cave can be enhanced with lighting systems.

George W. Mead Wildlife Area, Wisconsin

Willamette National Forest, Oregon

Olympic National Park, Washington

This moss-encrusted wooden bridge in the rain forest fits the landscape. A view to a sunny opening adds variety and interest to the scene.

A trail constructed in a long straight line, like over a man-made dike, is often monotonous and uninviting.

A curving trail over diverse topography is more appealing. The path invites visitors to explore.

The Trail Experience

"The essence of [nature guiding] is to travel gracefully rather than arrive."

Enos Mills
Adventures of a Nature Guide, 1920

Successful trails blend mystery, variety, and beauty into a holistic experience. A well-designed trail helps to facilitate meaningful connections between visitors and the landscape.

Trails don't just lead to places; they are places. A good trail should invite us to explore beyond each bend, pause and contemplate vistas, and engage our minds and imaginations.

At its best, a trail helps us to understand not only a place, but perhaps something about ourselves.

Dunnottar Castle, Scotland

The winding walk to Dunnottar Castle in Scotland is filled with anticipation. The castle stands on rock between land and sea. When you pass through its gateway, you transition into an ancient world of history, myth, and spirit.

The well-maintained trail provides stunning vistas of the castle, rolling landscape, and roaring shoreline. The ancient stone structures glow orange in the setting sun, adding to the mystery and spirit of the site.

Designing for Mystery, Variety, and Beauty

Each trail should provide a unique and refreshing adventure. Trail planning is much more than putting a path through the woods. It is a holistic endeavor that includes an understanding of the needs of people and the potential of the site. While the trail's purpose is to provide an opportunity for movement, the "view" from the trail is paramount to a rewarding experience.

• Create a trailhead as an inviting gateway that promises potential users safe, informative, and fun experiences.

• Design a trail entrance that offers glimpses of what can be seen on the trail, but conceals some mysteries that lie ahead.

• Route trails past the largest trees.

• Manage vegetation for diversity in texture, patterns, and density.

• Introduce or maintain colorful trees, shrubs, and ground covers.

• Plan vistas that allow directed views to lakes, peaks, valleys, and cliffs.

• Create views into forests and other vegetation (selectively cut understory, prune lower branches, thin stands, and create openings). Don't overdo this, however. Be sensitive to the natural form of vegetation and ecological integrity.

• Create forest openings that invite entry.

• Route the trail over running water and under large trees.

• Use structures to provide unique views and vistas.

• Use curves to draw people down trails.

• Screen objectionable views, sounds, or artificial structures.

• Position "views" on trails and boardwalks so the sun is on the visitor's back. This illuminates birds and other subjects for better viewing.

• Use landmarks, bridges, and distinct trail surfaces to assist visitors in wayfinding on the trail.

• Use materials for trail surfaces, signs, fences, benches, bridges, and other structures that are appropriately harmonious with the landscape and recreational experience.

Chapter 8:

Trail Construction and Maintenance

Schmeeckle Reserve, Wisconsin

A well-made and maintained trail must be in harmony with the landscape and be inviting and safe to users. The numbers of users and their activities determine choices in materials and maintenance procedures.

Trails can be classified into three broad functions: recreation, inter-pretation, and education. Some trails may be used for all three. Some uses are incompatible.

Categories of Use:	Recreation	Interpretation	Education
Activity Examples	• Motoring (scenic byway) • Horse-back riding (equestrian) • Off-road (ORV) motoring • Boating and canoeing • Bicycling and roller blading • Hiking • Fitness and jogging	• Orientation to an area • Self-guided learning about natural history • Self-guided learning about cultural history • Interpreter-guided learning about an area (trams and on foot)	• Study at designated trail stations • Use of trail as an outdoor classroom • Guided exploration involving sensory, conceptual, or factual information
Visitor Mode	Leisure Time Activities	Leisure Time Learning and Experiencing	Formal Learning

Green Circle Trail, Stevens Point, Wisconsin

Rogue Gorge, Rogue River National Forest, Oregon

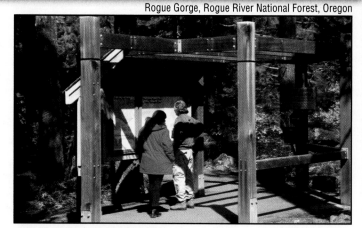

Recreational trails can be maintained for a single type of recreation or multiple uses.

Interpretive trails are designed to facilitate meaningful connections between the visitor and site.

Central Wisconsin Environmental Station, Wisconsin

Educational trails are often used in conjunction with non-formal learning programs, like camps, school forests, and nature centers.

Protecting the Trail Environment

Not every site should be invaded by trails. But, if a decision has been thoughtfully made, the next step is to lay out the trail with sensitivity and understanding of the site.

Keep in mind the purpose of the trail. Avoid over-construction. Most visitors to natural areas value a primitive appearance. A trail should never appear as an intrusion. It should follow the contours of the landscape and be surfaced with materials that blend with the site.

Erosion Control

Trail building starts by getting on your hands and knees. Look at your soil material. Find out what it is composed of and what it does in the rain. Find out where the water comes from before it gets to your trail and where it goes when it leaves. Your prime consideration is slowing and directing the water runoff from your trial surface.

Mark Edwards
Trails Coordinator, Iowa-DNR

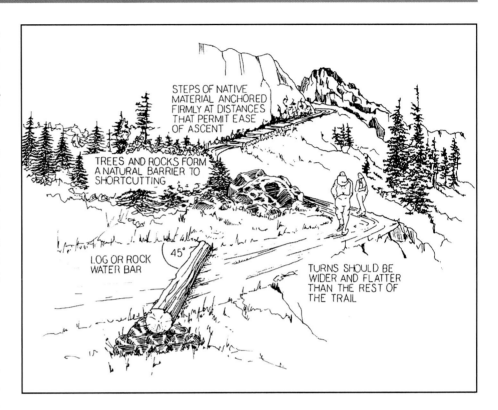

STEPS OF NATIVE MATERIAL ANCHORED FIRMLY AT DISTANCES THAT PERMIT EASE OF ASCENT

TREES AND ROCKS FORM A NATURAL BARRIER TO SHORTCUTTING

LOG OR ROCK WATER BAR

45°

TURNS SHOULD BE WIDER AND FLATTER THAN THE REST OF THE TRAIL

Constructing Trails on Slopes

A 0-5% (5% = 5 foot rise in 100 foot distance) grade is the most comfortable for walking. Inclines of more than 10% should be limited to short distances. Slopes over 7-10% will need steps, landings, and water bars to stop erosion. As you approach 50% you have passed the point of being able to control erosion.

An improperly surfaced trail *(left)* retains water. Trail "braiding" results when walkers avoid these wet areas.

Trails on slopes *(right)* can channel water and create gullies. These conditions must be corrected before severe damage results.

Protecting Wet and Fragile Areas

Some areas are best left inaccessible. Protect them from visitors by distance or visual screening.

Battle Creek Cypress Sanctuary, Maryland

Schmeeckle Reserve, Wisconsin

If the trail traverses fragile areas, such as ephemeral groundcovers or wetlands, line the trail with split rails or ropes. Elevated boardwalks also allow observation without entry.

Central Wisconsin Environmental Station, Wisconsin

Destructive Invaders

Trails open a site to more than human users. Some are destructive. Raccoons, cowbirds, skunks, and other predators gain access to other areas using man-made trails and roads. They can displace many native species. Consider the consequences a trail can have on fragile habitats.

Cutting of existing vegetation invites weedy invaders. Introducing sunlight where shade existed does the same. Revegetate with sun-loving native vegetation if this is a problem.

Trails become travel corridors for deer and other wildlife. By creating new entrances and exits, they may expand your trail system in unplanned ways.

Mammoth Cave National Park, Kentucky

Visitor Safety

Visitors seek the security of an identified trail. A trailhead, a sign, or map is an invitation to explore an area. Safety is not an amenity; it is a necessity and a legal obligation.

A well-designed trail should not become an "attractive nuisance." Dangerous cliffs, avalanche fields, high wind corridors, lightning prone ridges, or places prone to snowdrifting, bogging or iciness should be avoided.

If hazards cannot be avoided, then warning signs and protection must be provided.

Well informed visitors are capable of making decisions regarding their own well-being. Signs should set expectations and let users know the exact distances, difficulties, and alternatives they will encounter.

An old snag can become lethal in wind. Remove it if it threatens visitors on the trail.

Exposed roots and rocks can be dangerous to those who have diminished sight or mobility.

Maintenance

Maintenance Priorities

- Correct unsafe conditions.
- Prevent resource and trail damage.
- Provide for visitor convenience and comfort.

Trail Maintenance Documentation

Trail maintenance logs, people counters, and photo-documentation identify changing conditions.

Okefenokee National Wildlife Refuge, Georgia

An electric eye counts hikers as they break an invisible beam.

TRAIL LOG AND CONDITION/CORRECTION SURVEY
(from NPS Trails Management Handbook)

Park_____ Trail Name and No._____

Dist._____ Length_____ Page_____ of _____

Maint. Level:_____ Type of Trail:_____

Logged by:_____ | Surveyed by:_____

Date:_____ | Date:_____

Sta.	Feature	Condition/Correction	Equip.

Schmeeckle Reserve, Wisconsin

1980

2006

Documentation of trail changes can be accomplished by periodic photos from trail-side bench marks. These soon take on historic and scientific significance.

Trail Configuration

Interpretive Trails

Most visitors begin an interpretive walk at a parking lot or visitor center where they must return. A loop trail accomplishes this.

Loop Trail Advantages

- Visitors never see the same portion of the trail twice.
- A sense of solitude is enhanced since there are fewer encounters with other hikers.
- Only one trailhead is needed, reducing cost and maintenance.

Hiking Trails

Hiking trials may follow a multiple loop configuration. Since travel corridors are frequently linear, loops may not be feasible. Linear or horseshoe configurations may be the only options.

Small Group Teaching Trails

School groups and other educational groups are best accommodated by an orb-web design. Educational groups are typically divided into small teacher-led groups. Class periods require efficient travel to and from learning stations. Equal distances are desirable.

Central Wisconsin Environmental Station, Wisconsin

Central Wisconsin Environmental Station, Wisconsin

Trail Management Zones

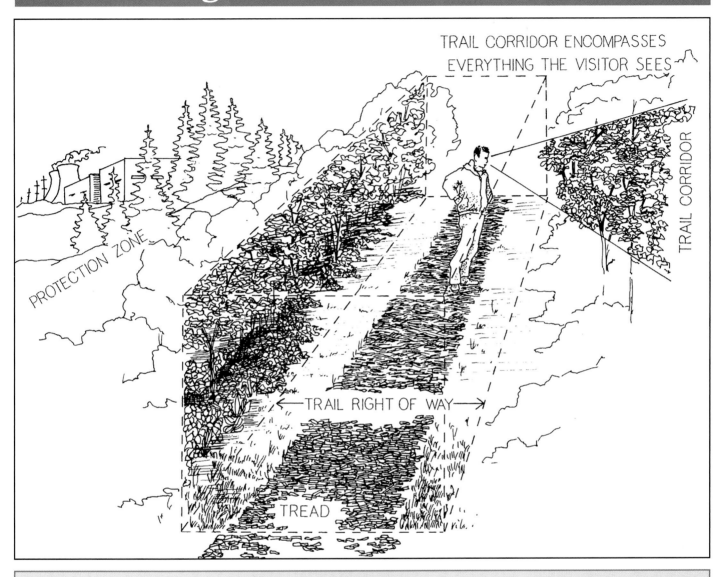

Definitions

- **Trail treadway or tread:** The surface the visitor walks on.

- **Trail right-of-way:** The area around the treadway that is cleared for safety.

- **Trail corridor:** The combination of the treadway, right-of-way, and all the land the visitor sees along the trail and that influences their perception of the trail.

- **Buffer or protection zone:** The land that insulates the hiker from activities adjacent to the trail that might be detrimental to the hiking experience including home development, mining, and logging. This zone can also serve to protect fragile areas from visitor damage.

Treadway

Trail surfaces affect the visitor visually, acoustically, and tactilely. When they work, trail surfaces go unnoticed; when they don't, they become the focus of frustration. Mud, unwanted noise, and unstable footing can ruin a walk experience even when the vistas are grand and wildlife is abundant. Trail surfaces are an unglamorous utilitarian feature fundamental to visitor needs—choose them carefully.

Trail surface materials are determined by:
- Amount of visitor use
- Characteristics of the substrate
- Aesthetic compatibility with the site
- Cost

Generally, more traffic demands more resilient surfaces. Main trails, such as those connecting visitor centers to parking lots, might require asphalt or crushed rock. If your site experiences spring melt or high groundwater, a boardwalk could be a necessity. A short loop trail through a small meadow might only need mowing to accommodate a few visitors. Bird watchers seeking solitude may prefer little more than a pruned game trail that discourages group use.

Surface	Applications	Advantages	Disadvantages	Suggestions
Asphalt (epoxy/sand coating provides a rough surface that prevents slipping)	Heavy Use Wheelchair Accessible	Little maintenance.	High initial cost. Often looks unnatural. Expensive. Subject to cracking. Tacky in hot sun.	Allow vegetation to grow over edges for natural appearance and coat surface with an epoxy/sand mixture.
Soil Cement (cement mixed with local parent material like gravel)	Heavy Use Wheelchair Accessible	More visually appealing than asphalt.	Expensive.	Crown slightly for drainage.
Paving Stones	Heavy Use	Allows water for infiltration. Attractive surface.	Installation labor intensive. Expensive.	Use mechanical vibrator to set stones.
Gravel (limestone/granite)	Heavy Use	Inexpensive. Allows for water infiltration.	Noisy. Not good for wildlife observation trails.	Weeds invade if a deep layer is not applied.
Woodchips	Medium Use	Natural appearance. Easy application.	Can become soggy in poorly drained areas. Require replenishment.	Hardwood chips are most desirable. Avoid material with sharp and angular chunks due to dull chipping machines.
Shredded Bark	Low/Medium Use	Visually appealing/natural, soft surface.	Breaks down quickly. Only available near saw mills.	Effective in dry areas. Preferred by runners and joggers.
Grass	Low Seasonal Use	Aesthetically appealing in open areas.	Requires a recovery period.	Use where alternative routes allow recovery.
Natural Surface	Wilderness/Low Use	Minimal maintenance.	Can easily degenerate into fragments and braided trails.	Use markers and maps.

Universal Design Considerations

Whenever possible, consider ways of making trails accessible to people of varying physical abilities. **Hard surfaces** allow access for most visitors. Trails should include a **gutter** on one side and a **kickboard** on the other to aid the visually impaired. Wheelchairs require grades of less than **1 foot rise to every 18 feet**. A minimum **5-foot** width allows two wheelchairs to pass.

Trail Surfaces

Glacier National Park, Montana

Glacier National Park, Montana

Heavily used trails may actually appear more natural when an appropriate hard surface is chosen. They resist erosion and are accessible to most visitors.

Schmeeckle Reserve, Wisconsin

Schmeeckle Reserve, Wisconsin

Woodchips fit a forest environment.

Keeweenaw Peninsula, Michigan

Locally quarried stone on a frequently wet trail provides a non-skid surface.

Schmeeckle Reserve, Wisconsin

Grass may be sufficient where traffic is seasonal or light.

Wood blocks *(left)* are covered with wire mesh to prevent slipping on a perpetually wet trail.

Monte Verde Preserve, Costa Rica

Schmeeckle Reserve, Wisconsin

This simple boardwalk protects a vernal wet woods.

Trail Corridor Management

This right-of-way lacks visual interest.

The undulating pattern of this right-of-way cut adds visual interest.

A more intricate pattern of vegetation adds mystery and variety to a walker's view.

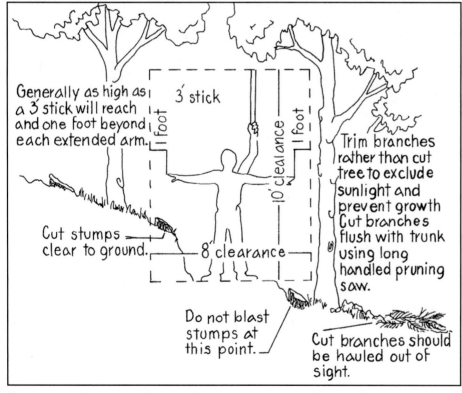

Generally as high as a 3' stick will reach and one foot beyond each extended arm.

3' stick

1 foot

10' clearance

1 foot

Trim branches rather than cut tree to exclude sunlight and prevent growth Cut branches flush with trunk using long handled pruning saw.

Cut stumps clear to ground.

8' clearance

Do not blast stumps at this point.

Cut branches should be hauled out of sight.

Suggested clearance for an interpretive trail. This will accommodate two people walking side by side.

Schmeeckle Reserve, Wisconsin

Trails maintained for high use require vehicle access and must be 5-6 feet wide for utility vehicles and 8-10 for trucks.

Trail Structures

Well-designed structures can add to the charm and usability of a trail. Structures should be built in harmony with the site, enhancing the holistic trail experience. Design and construction books are listed in the Resources section.

Seating

Well-placed benches invite visitors to pause, reflect, or observe nature. They can be a simple log, split log, or a construction of lumber.

Schmeeckle Reserve, Wisconsin

Beinn Eighe National Nature Reserve, Scotland

Consider creative seating options that help enhance the beauty, variety, and mystery of your trail while reinforcing interpretive themes.

The diversity of bench designs at Beinn Eighe National Nature Reserve in Scotland reflect the "Scot's pine" theme of the trail.

Bridges

Water crossings can be as unobtrusive as a culvert or have as much character as a suspension bridge.

Capilano Suspension Bridge, Canada

Hiawatha National Forest, Michigan

Structures, like this suspension bridge, can be a welcome change in elevation and treadway.

Swinging bridges offer a sense of adventure, but can limit accessibility.

Knockan Crag National Nature Reserve, Scotland

Schmeeckle Reserve, Wisconsin

Multnomah Falls, Oregon

A curving rail adds elegance and invites visitors to peer over the edge.

A rustic bridge with solid wood planks and log rails is ideal in a natural area.

The proper placement and creative design of a bridge can enhance the aesthetics and drama of a site.

Boardwalks

Boardwalks over wetland areas keep feet dry, protect sensitive habitats, and provide universal access to hard-to-reach areas. When elevated, they give a fresh perspective. Railings are an important safety element on elevated boardwalks, but may limit viewing for children or people in wheelchairs. At times, a low bumper along the edge may be more effective.

Everglades National Park, Florida

Glacier National Park, Montana

An elevated boardwalk on the Mahogany Trail takes visitors into the treetops.

This cedar takes on special significance when incorporated into the boardwalk.

Corkscrew Swamp Audubon Sanctuary, Florida

Rocky Mountain National Park, Colorado

A bald cypress swamp is accessible only on this mile-long boardwalk. This internationally renowned trail is a favorite haunt of naturalists and photographers.

Motorists on Trail Ridge Road can pull over and walk a short boardwalk for a close view of a beaver pond.

Viewing Blinds

The opportunity to see wildlife is a strong incentive to explore a trail. Blinds help to conceal human activity, allowing animals to be more comfortable around the structure. They serve as ideal observation areas for viewing wildlife up-close.

Designing with indigenous natural materials not only enhances the blind's camouflaging effect, but also makes it more aesthetically pleasing and inviting for visitors.

Bell Slough Wildlife Management Area, Arkansas

Six Mile Cypress Slough Preserve, Florida

Leafy vines growing on a fence conceal visitors from wildlife in the slough. A viewing scope peers through a hole in the fence.

A blind can be as simple as a few boards attached horizontally across an opening. This effectively breaks up the human form.

Crowley's Ridge Nature Center, Arkansas

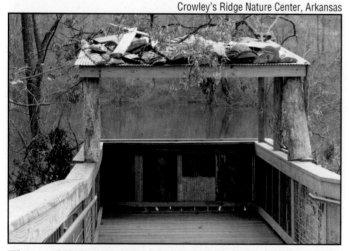

Santa Anna National Wildlife Refuge, Texas

This wildlife viewing blind was constructed to look like a duck hunter's blind, following the theme of the nature center.

A roof over the blind invites visitors to explore, and encourages viewing even in inclement weather.

Towers and Observation Platforms

Visitors are naturally attracted to structures that rise above their normal viewing height. Towers and platforms allow people to see the site from a different perspective and allow for much greater viewing distances. They can reveal wildlife that might otherwise be difficult to see on the ground. Structures must be carefully designed to minimize liability and reduce the aesthetic impact on the landscape.

Ding Darling National Wildlife Refuge, Florida

Ramps should be used when possible to make portions of a tower universally accessible.

Everglades National Park, Florida

Wading birds, often concealed by pond vegetation, are more easily seen from this elevated platform. An interpretive panel on the rail helps viewers to identify common birds of Eco Pond.

Okefenokee National Wildlife Refuge, Georgia

Towers offer an opportunity to witness natural phenomena from a birds-eye-view.

Okefenokee National Wildlife Refuge, Georgia

Viewing scopes help to bring wildlife observations closer and offer different perspectives of the site. This tower in Okefenokee National Wildlife Refuge reveals alligators bellowing during the mating season.

Chapter 9:
Trail Interpretation

Recreational development is a job not of building roads into lovely country, but of building receptivity into the still unlovely human mind.

Aldo Leopold
A Sand County Almanac

Big Bend National Park, Texas

Civilization has removed people from firsthand experiences. A trail experience can be a sensory, intellectual, and emotional immersion. A person on a trail is rediscovering his or her roots and place on the earth. In the process, they are learning about themselves.

Interpretation should assist in this discovery. The challenge to interpreters is to help people find meaning in these experiences. It is a formidable challenge, but the highest purpose of a natural or cultural site is to help people realize their connection to the resource.

Since everyone experiences something different on a trail, a personal visit with an interpreter is a good way to help them find meaning. Nothing beats person-to-person interpretation.

However, since we cannot spend time with every visitor, we must rely on alternatives.

	Mode of Interpretation	Advantages	Disadvantages
Personal and Spontaneous Interpretation	**Interpreter-led walk**	Personal interaction is the most effective way to develop themes and stories.	Relatively few contacts. Some group members may not "tune in." Expensive.
	Roving interpreter on trail	Most individualized form of interpretation.	Frequently only information is provided, not insight. Usually limited to brief encounters.
Non-personal and Inflexible Interpretation	**General appreciation booklet or pamphlet**	Can be read before or after hiking the trail. A detailed story can be told through graphics and text. No impact on the site.	Does not provide specific information about what is being immediately experienced and cannot answer questions the visitor may have.
	Leaflet and marker	The only physical imposition on the site is a numbered or symboled post. An effective technique for auto tours.	Reading literature while standing on a nature trail is unnatural. Leaflet can become litter.
	Wayside exhibits	Available to all visitors whenever the site is open. Interprets objects or site directly. Flexibility exists to change individual signs.	They are a physical imposition on the site. Initially expensive. Subject to vandalism. Require reading by standing visitors.
	Audio trails	A human voice allows first person interpretation to humanize story. It is easier to listen than to read. Often a good choice for cultural interpretation.	Require specialized equipment and professional production to be effective.

Alternatives for Trail Interpretation

Guided Walks and Roving Interpretation

Apostle Islands National Lakeshore, Wisconsin

If staffing permits, this is the best choice for trail interpretation.

"Next to the real thing, people in face to face communication are best, and there are a number of ways that spoken words from living lips can interpret."

Yorke Edwards
The Land Speaks

General Appreciation Publication

A well-designed and well-written general brochure about a site or trail allows visitors to learn at a convenient time.

If distributed at an entrance station or visitor center, there is no sign, marker, or leaflet box to mar the landscape. Publications communicate beyond the confines of the park. They can be read in the living room, car, or campsite.

Leaflet and Marker

Rocky Mountain National Park, Colorado

Big Bend National Park, Texas

Rocky Mountain National Park, Colorado

Leaflet and marker walking trails are seldom the most effective techniques for interpreting a site. The written word is not the story. The story surrounds the visitor. It is unnatural to read an abstract message as you venture down a real trail full of happenings. Visitor observation has documented that few people read publications on a trail.

Leaflet and marker interpretation is often successfully used for car touring. The *Trail Ridge Road Guide* in Rocky Mountain National Park is popular with motorists visiting the park. Graphically appealing, it uses active, engaging text to share the story of Trail Ridge Road.

Techniques for Leaflet and Marker Interpretation

• Have a **theme** that unifies the story and sounds exciting.

• Use **provocative titles** at each station.

• Write **concise and exciting inscriptions** for each stop.

• **Limit interpretation** to the minimum number of stations needed to tell the story. Visitors soon tire of this medium. (The *Trail Ridge Road Guide* has 12 stops, an optimal number.)

• Incorporate **strong graphics and illustrations** to help tell the story.

Head-Smashed-In Buffalo Jump, Alberta, Canada

Trail Wayside Exhibits

"Let's free the hands of the visitors, so their eyes, nose, and ears can be attuned to the actual on-site experiences."

Tanner Pilley
NPS Interpretive Media Specialist

Wayside exhibits are frequently used for trail interpretation. The signs can be constructed in a variety of media, incorporate graphics, and be placed next to the features being interpreted. A word of caution: they still require the visitor to read while standing. Signs also impose on the landscape. A significant number of people must use the trail to justify the expense and upkeep of a sign.

If, after careful consideration, you choose to interpret with trail signage, adherence to basic principles can increase effectiveness. Chapters 2-6 provide a detailed treatment of these principles. Additional tips are included in the box below.

Techniques for Effective Trail Wayside Exhibits

- Have an **inviting trailhead** that includes an **engaging trail name**.

- Use an **introductory sign** to set the theme of the trail and indicate trail length. This sign usually has a longer message. On some trails, this may be the only interpretation needed or desired.

- All signs should have a **provocative title, graphics, and minimal text.**

- Incorporate **audio and interactive devices** to maximize effective communication.

- Many interpretive sign specialists recommend that the **majority of interpretive signs be placed early on the trail** while the visitor is still fresh and interested. Avoid placing two signs in view of each other.

- Place signs at **natural stopping points** and where people have questions.

- **Limit signs** to maintain visitor interest.

- **Common trail panel sizes** are 30"x18" for major panels and 7"x5" for identification panels. They should be mounted at a 30-45° angle to the ground (recommendations by Tanner Pilley).

- Signs should be placed to **avoid ruining pristine areas and scenic views.**

Case Studies in Trail Interpretation

Tijeras Pueblo Archaeological Site

The Tijeras Pueblo in the Cibola National Forest of New Mexico is a 600 year old village site once occupied by Puebloan people. Although little can be seen above the surface, the site is a treasure trove of information for archaeologists who work to unravel the lives of the people who lived here.

The U.S. Forest Service has created a hands-on discovery trail that helps facilitate connections between modern-day visitors and the past inhabitants.

Tijeras Pueblo Archaeological Site, Cibola National Forest, New Mexico

The trailhead introduces the theme of the hike, both visually and in its message. A concise map indicates trail length, hiking time, accessibility, and warnings.

The panels are made of porcelain enamel, which prevents fading from the harsh sun. The wood backing and subtle coloration blend well with the arid environment.

The trail is made of hard compacted dirt and gravel. It is low maintenance and accessible to people with wheelchairs or strollers.

Smaller plant identification panels are unified with the main exhibits, but made of etched metal.

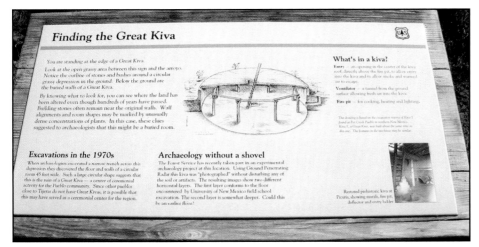

Several tactile models of Pueblo buildings that once stood on the site are located along the trail. Adjacent wayside exhibits interpret the function of each building.

Visitors are encouraged to touch real objects, like this bedrock *metate*, a smooth depression created from grinding seeds and nuts.

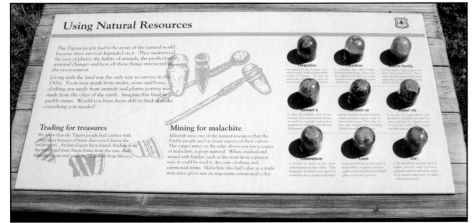

Viewing tubes focus a visitor's attention on a copper mine dug by the Pueblo inhabitants. Clear resin molds mounted to the panel surface hold real samples of turquoise, malachite, and other mined minerals.

Golden Gate Canyon State Park

A stream-fed trout pond serves as the focal point for this interpretive trail loop. A paved trail leads visitors to wayside exhibits which tell the story of a mountain stream ecosystem.

Bridges with low railings offer intimate views of the babbling trout stream.

The short trail loop adjacent to the visitor center introduces people to the site in a comfortable way.

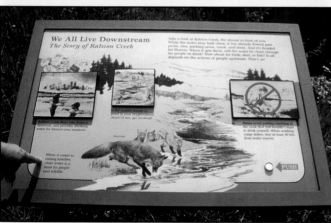

Raised high pressure laminate panels and audio messages narrated by a young girl encourage exploration.

Tactile elements add dimension and opportunities for multi-sensory experiences.

Sugarlands Valley Nature Trail

Sugarlands Valley Nature Trail, Great Smoky Mountains National Park, Tennessee

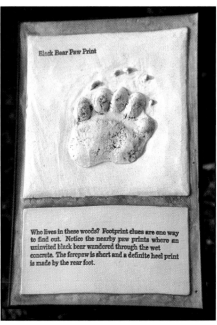

This nature trail in Great Smoky Mountains National Park demonstrates several examples of universal accessibility. Bridges blend seamlessly with the trail surface and incorporate benches for seating.

Imprinted ceramic panels engage tactile learners and people with visual impairments.

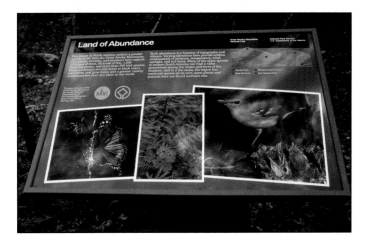

A hard trail surface, angled panels, and benches *(upper left)* accommodate people of many physical abilities.

Porcelain enamel panels *(above)* incorporate photographs that communicate in a universal language. High contrast makes the text more readable.

The parking lot and trailhead *(left)* are accessible to everyone.

Cactus Garden Trail

Cactus Garden Trail, Saguaro National Park, Arizona

Adjacent to a visitor center in Saguaro National Park, this trail introduces visitors to desert plants.

A paved meandering path provides easy access into the arid environment, while adding mystery to the trail.

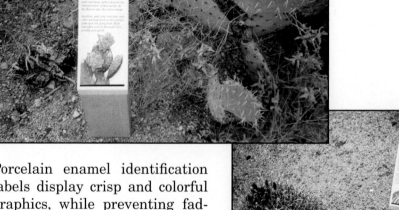

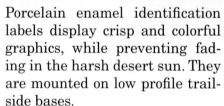

Porcelain enamel identification labels display crisp and colorful graphics, while preventing fading in the harsh desert sun. They are mounted on low profile trailside bases.

Beaver Meadows Boardwalk

The Beaver Meadows Boardwalk in Rocky Mountain National Park leads visitors through active beaver ponds and dams. Wayside exhibits interpret beaver adaptations and behaviors.

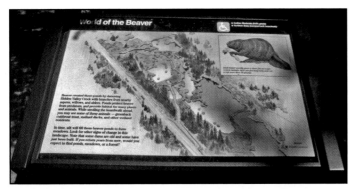

A trailhead sign near the parking area orients and prepares visitors to walk the boardwalk loop.

Enticing visuals and dramatic text on porcelain enamel panels convey meanings to people experiencing the sights, smells, and sounds of the site.

"The Construction Zone" panel interprets the area of a dam actively being rebuilt by beavers.

A well-designed and aesthetically pleasing walkway invites adventure.

Personal Audio Tours

Voices and sounds can make a site come alive for visitors. Lightweight, small, and user-friendly handheld devices offer CD-quality sound and ample storage for thousands of interpretive messages. The units can accommodate multiple languages, be activated by the user or by infrared beams, and even collect statistics on visitor usage.

An audio tour specialist or experienced AV consultant can help select the most appropriate technology. Generally, headset systems are best used indoors or at historical sites because natural areas provide their own sounds. (Production Tips for Audio Messages can be found on page 59.)

Alcatraz Island Federal Correction Facility, California

Almost one million visitors annually take the audio tour at Alcatraz. Players are stored in recharging units when not in use.

Audio narration and exhibit panels tell the story of prison life on "Broadway," the main courtyard of the prison.

Alcatraz Cellhouse Tour

Visitors to Alcatraz Island Federal Correctional Facility in San Francisco learn what it was like to live and work on the island. Events at Alcatraz from 1934 to 1963 are recreated on a 43 minute tour using tape narration and a rechargeable, portable cassette player.

Former correctional officers narrate this award winning tour. Former inmates tell their stories about life on the cellblock. Photos and graphics at each stop give faces to the voices on the tape. Sound effects (the clanging of cell doors, harmonicas at night, the whistles of guards, battle sounds from the 1947 prison riot) bring the story to life.

Graceland Mansion Tour

Graceland Mansion, Tennessee

Graceland Mansion in Memphis, Tennessee was the home of Elvis Presley for 21 years. An audio tour is an ideal way to connect visitors to Elvis' personal life. His songs serve as a background to the narration, and actual interviews bring his story to life.

Visitors punch codes into the audio device to hear different messages, allowing people to choose the depth of interpretation.

U.S.S. Bowfin Submarine Tour

U.S.S. Bowfin Submarine Museum, Hawaii

A wand radio system triggers messages as visitors explore this World War II submarine, now a National Historic Landmark. Battle sounds and first-person accounts bring to life the nine wartime patrols of this sub and its 80-man crew.

Gettysburg Battlefield Driving Tour

Gettysburg National Military Park, Pennsylvania

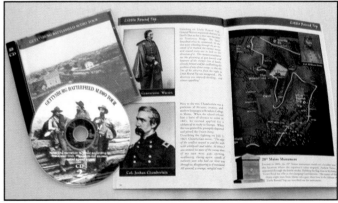

Nearly every automobile has a CD or tape player, providing a unique opportunity for personal audio interpretation when touring a large area. The Gettysburg Battlefield Audio Tour guides visitors with Civil War music, dramatic sound effects, and an engaging narrative. A corresponding booklet includes maps and images that augment the audio message.

Resources

Big Bend National Park, Texas

Photograph/ Illustration Credits

All photographs in this book were taken by the Schmeeckle Reserve Interpreters team of Dr. Michael Gross, Ron Zimmerman, and Jim Buchholz unless otherwise listed below.

Inside front cover: Schmeeckle Reserve boardwalk. Courtesy of Doug Moore.

Chapter 2, p. 13: Boulder Creek sign. Courtesy of ECOS Communications.

Chapter 2, p. 15: Fort Sumpter cannon. Courtesy of Paul Trapp.

Chapter 2, p. 15: Glacier Bay National Park canoe and sign. Courtesy of Chuck Lennox.

Chapter 2, p. 24: Mosquito Hill Trails sign. Courtesy of Jim Anderson.

Chapter 2, p. 28-29: Hells Canyon kiosks and signs. Courtesy of Jane Rohling.

Chapter 3, p. 34: Montezuma Castle sign illustration. Courtesy of Tanner Pilley.

Chapter 3, p. 36: Miami Metro Zoo sign. Courtesy of Paul Trapp.

Chapter 3, p. 36: Western Springs Lakeside sign. Courtesy of Raymond Tabata.

Chapter 3, p. 36: Creatures of the Night sign. Courtesy of ECOS Communications.

Chapter 3, p. 39: The Proper Ingredients sign. Courtesy of Missouri Department of Conservation.

Chapter 3, p. 41: Gray's Lake National Wildlife Refuge sign. Courtesy of Wilderness Graphics, Inc.

Chapter 3, p. 46: Saguaro National Park sign. Courtesy of the National Park Service.

Chapter 4, p. 51: Chatfield State Park sign. Courtesy of ECOS Communications.

Chapter 4, p. 52: Arches National Park sign. Courtesy of the National Park Service.

Chapter 4, p. 53: Denver Zoo sign. Courtesy of ECOS Communications.

Chapter 4, p. 68: Montezuma Castle sign illustration. Courtesy of Tanner Pilley.

Chapter 5, p. 72: The Falkirk Wheel HPL panel. Courtesy of iZone.

Chapter 5, p. 73: Chesapeake Bay Gateway fiberglass sign. Courtesy of Pannier Graphics.

Chapter 5, p. 74: George Washington Birthplace porcelain enamel sign. Courtesy of the National Park Service.

Chapter 5, p. 75: Color-Embedded Anodized Aluminum signs. Courtesy of ALUimage.

Chapter 5, p. 76: Photo-Chemically Etched Anodized Aluminum signs. Courtesy of Interpretive Graphics.

Chapter 5, p. 79: Routed/carved wooden St. Francis's Trail sign. Courtesy of Nancy Cripe.

Chapter 5, p. 80: Sandblasting process. Courtesy of 3M Corporation.

Chapter 5, p. 81: Municipal Dock back-screened Lexan. Courtesy of Genesis Graphics.

Chapter 5, p. 82: Anza Borrego State Park stone signs. Courtesy of Stone Imagery.

Chapter 5, p. 82: Miami Metro Zoo cast ceramic. Courtesy of Suzanne Trapp.

Chapter 5, p. 87: Cape Pepetua Scenic Area supports. Courtesy of Dahn Design.

Chapter 5, p. 88: Arches National Park sign. Courtesy of the National Park Service.

Chapter 5, p. 91: Moody Air Force Base kiosk. Courtesy of Wilderness Graphics.

Chapter 6, p. 103: Mount Saint Helens visitors reading sign. Courtesy of Dahn Design.

Chapter 6, p. 103: Mount Saint Helens signs. Courtesy of USDA Forest Service.

Chapter 8, p. 122: Green Circle Trail skiing. Courtesy of Linda Wenzl.

Chapter 8, p. 122: Educational trail. Courtesy of the Central Wisconsin Environmental Station.

Chapter 8, p. 124: Battle Creek Cypress Sanctuary boardwalk. Courtesy of Dwight Williams.

Chapter 8, p. 131: Glacier National Park trail. Courtesy of Alan Capelle.

Chapter 8, p. 131: Schmeeckle Reserve grass trail. Courtesy of Dennis Chapman.

Chapter 8, p. 137: Everglades National Park sign. Courtesy of Paul Trapp.

Chapter 9, p. 147: Sugarlands Valley Nature Trail. Courtesy of Great Smoky Mountains National Park.

Chapter 9, p. 150: Alcatraz Cellhouse Tour photos. Courtesy of Chris Tellis, Antenna Audio.

Book Resources

There are many books to choose from when designing interpretive signs, trails, and wayside exhibits. These are some of the most useful.

Accessibility Standards

Americans with Disabilities Act Handbook
U.S. Employment Opportunity Commission and the U.S. Justice Dept., October, 1992

Interpretation for Disabled Visitors in the National Park System
David Park, Wendy Ross, W. Ellis
National Park Service, Washington D.C., 1984
U.S. Government Printing Office, Washington, DC 20402

See National Park Service web site for 1999 document on accessibility for interpretive media.
www.nps.gov/hfc/products/waysides/

Signs and Wayside Exhibits

Architectural Signing and Graphics
John Follis and Dave Hamer
Whitney Library of Design, Watson-Guptill Publications, New York, NY, 1988

Environmental Interpretation: A Practical Guide for People with Big Ideas and Small Budgets
Sam H. Ham
North American Press, Golden, CO, 1992

The Graphics of Communication
Turnbull and R. Baird
4th Ed., New York, NY, 1980

Exhibit Labels: An Interpretive Approach
Beverly Serrell
Alta Mira Press, Walunut Cree, CA, 1996

Making Wood Signs
Patrick Spielman
Sterling Publishing Co., Inc., New York, NY, 1981

Noah's Art: Zoo, Aquarium, Aviary and Wildlife Park Graphics
Edited by Wei Yew
Quon Editions, Edmonton, Alberta, Canada, 1991

The Non-Designers Design Book: Design and Typographic Principles for the Visual Novice
Robin Williams
Peachpit Press, Berkeley, California, 2004

An essential guide for anyone working with design and type. Visually introduces basic design principles.

Wayfinding: Designing and Implementing Graphic Navigational Systems
Craig Berger
RotoVision SA, East Sussex, England, 2005

Zoo Design: The Reality of Wild Illusions
Kenneth J. Polakowski
University of Michigan, Ann Arbor, MI, 1987

Trails

Complete Guide to Trail Building and Maintenance
Carl Demrow and David Salisbury
Appalachian Mountain Club Books, 3rd Ed., 1998
AMC's classic manual for planning, building, designing, and maintaining trails.

Greenways for America
Charles E. Little
Johns Hopkins University Press, Baltimore, MD, 1990
A philosophical treatise on green corridors with many case studies. Beautifully written and illustrated.

Lightly on the Land: The SCA Trail Building and Maintenance Manual
Robert C. Birkby
Mountaineers Books, 2nd Ed., 2006
Updated building and maintenance techniques from the Student Conservation Association.

NPS Trails Management Handbook
United States Department of the Interior, National Park Service, Denver Service Center, Denver, CO, 1994
US government Printing No. 576-279/85200

Trails for the Twenty-First Century: Planning, Design, and Management Manual for Multi-Use Trails
Charles A. Flink, Kristine Olka, and Robert M. Searns
Island Press, Washington D.C., 2001

Vandalism

Preventing Cultural Resources Destruction: Taking Action through Interpretation
Jan S. Ryan
Free distribution from National Park Service, 1992, Div. of Parks Historic Preservation, Western Regional Office, 600 Harrison St., San Francisco, CA 94107-1372, (415) 744-3961

Vandalism Control Management for Parks and Recreation Areas
Monty L. Christiansen
Venture Publishing, Inc., State College, PA, 1982
A complete vandalism control plan for recreation sites. Also see www.lib.niu.edu/ipo/1984/ip840120.html

Online Resources

Interpretive Organizations

University of Wisconsin-Stevens Point
"Schmeeckle Reserve"
www.uwsp.edu/schmeeckle

Interpretation resources maintained and updated by the authors of this book. Information for interpretation students and professionals. Topics include:
- Order the Interpreter's Handbook Series
- UWSP interpretive consulting and design services
- Rustic wooden sign fabrication
- Desktop publishing and digital presentation tutorials
- Information about the UWSP Environmental Education/Interpretation program
- Updated links to interpretive resources on the web

National Association for Interpretation (NAI)
www.interpnet.com

Professional organization dedicated to the advancement of interpretation with an emphasis on professional development and certification. Topics include:
- Calendar of events, including national and regional workshops
- Certification process and training programs
- Interpreter's Green Pages, listing of companies that offer interpretive services (see page 157)

Interpretation Canada
www.interpcan.ca

Professional organization that provides professional development activities, networking, and publications to enhance the development of theory and practice in the interpretive field. Topics include:
- Upcoming Events
- National Training Program
- Business Directory

Scottish Natural History
"Introducing Interpretation"
www.snh.org.uk/wwo/Interpretation/default.html

Concise and easy-to-read introduction to interpretive techniques. Topics include:
- Interpretive planning
- Writing effective interpretation
- Producing interpretive panels
- Making interpretation accessible to all
- Good practice guidelines

Signs and Wayside Exhibits

National Park Service
"Harpers Ferry Center"
www.nps.gov/hfc/products/waysides/

Comprehensive web site describing the National Park Service approach to planning, designing, and fabricating wayside exhibits. Topics include:
- Wayside Exhibit Work Process
- Why Use a Wayside Exhibit
- Preparing for a Planning/Design Contract
- Panels and Bases
- Installation and Maintenance
- Accessibility Guidelines
- Wayside Exhibit Gallery of Examples

Interpretive Signage: Principles and Practice
R. Ballantyne, K. Hughes & G. Moscardo
www.interpretivesigns.qut.edu.au/index.cfm

An overview of interpretive signage design, construction, and evaluation from the Queensland University of Technology. Several photographs of wayside exhibits illustrate the main points. Topics include:
- Interpretation and signage
- Attracting visitor's attention
- Selecting text and illustrations
- Constructing signs
- Evaluating signs

Trail Resources

Designing Sidewalks and Trails for Access
U.S. Department of Transportation, 1999
www.fhwa.dot.gov/environment/sidewalks/chap5a.htm

Publications on Trail Planning, Design, Construction, and Maintenance
Professional Trailbuilders Association
www.trailbuilders.org/resources/

Recreational Trail Design and Construction
David M. Rathke and Melvin J. Baughman, 2006
www.extension.umn.edu/distribution/naturalresources/DD6371.html

Trail Design, Building, and Maintenance Resources
Michael A. Neiger, 2002
therucksack.tripod.com/trailbuilding.htm

Planning, Design and Fabrication Companies

Companies Featured in this Book

The following companies contributed valuable information, photographs, and illustrations for the development of this book.

ALUimage
1017 Englewood Drive
Winston-Salem, NC 27106
336-724-9755
www.aluimage.com

Antenna Audio
1133 Broadway, Suite 321
New York, NY 10010
212-675-6191
www.antennaaudio.com

Dahn Design
3703 Walnut Ave. SW
Seattle, WA 98116
206-923-2853
www.dahndesign.com

ECOS Communications
2028 17th Street
Boulder, CO 80302
303-444-3267
www.ecos.us

Folia Industries Inc.
58 York, Huntington QC
Canada
J0S 1H0
888-264-6122
www.folia.ca

Genesis Graphics
1823 7th Av. N.
Escanaba, MI 49829
800-659-7734
www.genesisgraphicsinc.com

Interpretive Graphics
3590 Summerhill Drive
Salt Lake City, UT 84121
801-942-5812
www.InterpretiveGraphics.com

iZone
2526 Charter Oak Dr., Suite 100
Temple, TX 76502
888-464-9663
www.izoneimaging.com

Pannier Graphics
345 Oak Road
Gibsonia, PA 15044
800-544-8428 Ext: 220
www.panniergraphics.com

Schmeeckle Reserve Interpreters
2419 North Point Dr.
Stevens Point, WI 54481
715-346-4992
www.uwsp.edu/schmeeckle

Split Rock Studios
2071 Gateway Boulevard
St. Paul, MN 55112
800-433-9599
www.splitrockstudios.com

Stone Imagery
3546 Highland Drive
Carlsbad, CA 92008
760-434-4493
www.stoneimagery.com

Wilderness Graphics, Inc.
Post Office Box 1635
Tallahassee, FL 32302
850-224-6414
www.wildernessgraphics.com

Comprehensive Listings of Other Companies

The following online resources include comprehensive, up-to-date listings of planning, design, and fabrication companies.

National Association for Interpretation (NAI)
"Interpreter's Green Pages"
www.interpnet.com/greenpages/

- Audiovisual products
- Exhibit Fabrication, Services, and Supplies
- Graphic Design and Illustration
- Maps and Map Services
- Planning and Design
- Signage
- Writing

Association of Science-Technology Centers (ASTC)
"Products and Services"
www.astc.org/members/pslist/pslist.htm

- Display equipment
- Exhibit Fabrication
- Exhibit Planning and/or Design
- Multimedia/Audio/Visual Production Services
- Research and Evaluation

The America Zoo and Aquarium Association (AZA)
"AZA Commercial Members"
www.aza.org/FindCommercialMember/

- Designer
- Exhibits
- Master Planner
- Publisher
- Sculptor Artist
- Signage

Working with Designers and Fabricators

Define the project:

- Define your objectives and audiences.
- Write your objectives concisely.
- Determine what you will do yourself and what you will contract:
  - Research and develop concept.
  - Develop theme.
  - Develop outlines (one per panel).
  - Develop agency-approved bibliography which provides accurate information.
  - Develop a list of approved common and scientific names.
  - Collect first-person narratives and/or quotes.
  - Write inscriptions.
  - Produce art (drawings or photographs).

Working with a writer:

- Assign a project manager to handle all communications.
- Provide theme and outline.
- Provide agency-approved bibliography.
- Provide approved common and scientific names.
- Provide any first-person narratives or quotations.
- Provide maximum number of words per panel.
- Provide any specific safety, resource protection, and preservation information that should be included.
- Confirm in advance who has approval authority at each stage of the project and how many staff members must review and comment.
- Establish mutually agreed-upon time frames for submittal of each stage of work.
- Provide signed approval at each stage.
- Determine in advance how many revisions or rewrites will be covered in the contract.
- Specify in contract whether final is to be hard copy or digital.

Working with an illustrator/designer:

- Assign a project manager to handle all communications.
- Narrow the list of professional designers and fabricators to those that do the same type of work you want.
- Further narrow the list by talking to colleagues or references on the quality of the designer's services.
- Confirm that your final selections are interested in bidding on your work.
- Provide detailed information about your project to allow all interested parties to bid on your work. Communicate your decision-making criteria, specifications, timeline, and payment schedule.
- Make a written contract with the service provider. If your project is large or open-ended, be certain your contract is detailed.
- Confirm in advance who has approval authority at each stage and how many staff members must review and comment at each stage.
- Establish mutually agreed-upon time frames for submittal of each stage of work.
- Provide signed approval at each stage.
- Provide clear, detailed description of what is to be illustrated (provide photos, not other illustrations).
- If art is provided, specify in contract whether original art is to be returned to artist.
- Provide information on number of colors and method of fabrication.

Working with a fabricator:

- Have one person designated as the contact person for each party.
- Prior to signing your contract, make certain everyone's roles and responsibilities are clearly defined.
- Make sure colors are clearly specified with a universal color system (like PANTONE).
- Establish mutually agreed-upon time frames for production and delivery.
- Clear communication at each step of the process will eliminate wasted work and missed deadlines.

Index

A portion of the labor to produce this book
was kindly donated by

The Associates of
Worzalla Publishing Company
Stevens Point, Wisconsin

Celebrating 20 years
of 100% employee ownership
1986 – 2006

WORZALLA